The Sieges of Derry

William Kelly

Editor

FOUR COURTS PRESS

Set in 10.5 on 12.5 point Ehrhardt for
Four Courts Press Ltd
Fumbally Lane, Dublin 8, Ireland
e-mail: info@four-courts-press.ie
and in North America
Four Courts Press
c/o ISBS, 5824 N.E. Hassalo Street, Portland, OR 97213

A catalogue record for this title
is available from the British Library

ISBN 1–85182–510–X

Printed in Great Britain
by MPG Books, Bodmin, Cornwall

Contents

Chronology

1688

23 November	Mountjoy's regiment recalled and leaves Derry. Public meetings held.
6 December	Comber letter arrives in Derry. Earl of Antrim arrives at Limavady. Fears of massacres in the city.
7 December	Redshanks arrive. Apprentice Boys close the gates against them. Magazine seized.
8 December	Bishop Hopkins leaves the city. Most of Catholic population expelled from the city.
9 December	Earl of Antrim approaches Derry.
11 December	David Cairns leaves to seek assistance at London.
12 December	Mountjoy and Lundy arrive back with his regiment. Townspeople refuse admission to Catholic soldiers but admit two companies of Protestants. Colonel Lundy appointed governor.
15 December	Sir Arthur Rawdon and Lord Mountalexander garrison Coleraine with 4,000 men.
18 December	William of Orange arrives in London. James II flees to France.
20 December	Captain James Hamilton arrives from England with money and arms and ammunition for 2,000 men. He carries a commission for Lundy from William and Mary appointing him governor. Captain Hamilton administers the oath of fidelity to Their Majesties to all officers, civil and military. Lundy takes the oath privately.
21 December	William and Mary proclaimed in the city. Agreement reached that Lundy remains as governor even though he refused to publicly take the oath of fidelity.

1689

2 January	Committee set up to purchase arms.
17 January	Council of Northern Gentry formed at Hillsborough.
13 February	William and Mary proclaimed by English parliament. Richard Hamilton advancing on Ulster.
21 February	Attempt by Council of Northern gentry to seize Carrickfergus fails.
7 March	Proclamation issued by Lord-Lieutenant Richard Talbot stigmatising Northern gentry as rebels and accusing them

	of murdering His Majesty's subjects. Ten principal gentry excluded from pardon.
12 March	James II lands at Kinsale. Richard Talbot created duke of Tyrconnel.
14 March	Break of Dromore. Sir Arthur Rawdon's troops routed by Richard Hamilton.
21 March	*Deliverance* arrives with supplies including 8,000 muskets, 480 barrels of powder and money and a new commission for Lundy. (Only for the arrival of these arms the city could not have been defended.) Declaration of Union issued in the city. Signed by the officers and Committee of Londonderry they pledged to defend the city against the Jacobites.
22 March	Ceremony to publicly proclaim William and Mary.
24 March	James I enters Dublin in state procession.
27 March	Jacobite forces invest and attack Coleraine. Repulsed. James I decides to send main body of army to the north.
8 April	James II leaves Dublin for the North. Williamite forces retreat from Coleraine and County Derry to assemble in Londonderry.
10 April	Cairns arrives back from London. Letter from King William informs the governor and council that forces for their relief are already at sea. Council of War discusses defence of city. Engagement to defend the city to the last.
13 April	Death of Mayor. New Mayor Gervais Squire. Jacobite forces appear in the Waterside (east bank of river Foyle) en route from Coleraine to the fords at Clady and Lifford. Jacobites fire a cannon at the city. George Walker arrives in the city with news of large Jacobite force heading for Derry. Commanded by Rosen. Council of War decides to defend the fords and passes. James II at Omagh.
14 April	James II, at St Johnston, sends the earl of Abercorn to Derry to offer terms. His offer is rejected.
15 April	Jacobite dragoons under the command of General Rosen cross the river. Williamites flee in disarray back to Derry. Williamite reinforcements commanded by Colonels Cunningham and Richards arrive in Lough Foyle.
16 April	Council of War. Deciding the city is untenable, the two newly arrived regiments set sail for England. (They remained in Lough Foyle until 19 April).
17 April	James II, at Charlemont, receives news of Jacobite successes at Lifford and Cladyford. Decides to go to Derry.

18 April	Lundy leaves. Rev. George Walker and Henry Baker suggested as joint governors. James II appears before the walls. Fired on by the defenders. At Murray's instigation it seems.
19 April	George Walker and Henry Baker appointed joint governors.
20 April	Adam Murray parlays with the earl of Abercorn. Jacobites occupy Carrigans and St Johnston.
21 April	First major action. Defenders attack the Jacobites at Pennyburn Mill. French commander of the Jacobites, Maumont, killed, allegedly by Adam Murray.
23 April	Culmore Fort surrenders to the Jacobites. (Rumours were rife in the city that it had been betrayed by 'two of the Adairs and long Galbraith the attorney.') City shelled from Stronge's orchard in the Waterside.
24 April	Only about 30 rounds fired between this date and 4 May.
25 April	Skirmish at Pennyburn mill. General Pusignan killed. Richard Hamilton now the senior surviving Jacobite officer.
5 May	Jacobites under Brigadier Ramsey move to capture Windmill Hill.
6 May	Jacobites capture the Windmill to the south of the city.
7 May	Defenders recapture Windmill. James II leaves for Dublin. Parliament meets in Dublin. Act of Attainder condemns 2,400 Protestants as rebels and forfeits their estates. Acts of Settlement and Explanation repealed.
15 May	Disagreements between the officers commanding in the city. Governor Baker wounds Colonel Mitchelburne in a dispute. The latter confined to his quarters.
16 May	Several citizens parley with the Jacobites on their own initiative. They are fired on from the city.
17 May	Reinforcements for Derry under Major-General Kirke sail from Liverpool.
18 May	Skirmishing at Creggan. Besieged drive Jacobite infantry from the fort. Attacked by Jacobite cavalry. Captain John Cunningham and sixteen others slain.
30 May	Jacobite couriers are intercepted en route to Dublin. Correspondence reveals 3,000 officers and men already dead from illness and military action. On this same day the defenders hear of relief fleet sailing from England. Morale in the city is boosted.
May, last week	Jacobites construct a boom across the river stretching from Charles fort to Grange fort. Skirmishing at Pennyburn and at the Windmill.

1 June	The *Greyhound*, sent by Major-General Kirke to assess the situation, arrives in Lough Foyle.
2 June	Jacobites recommence firing into city. Rosen arrives with fresh troops.
3 June	Defenders see four ships in Lough Foye. Jacobite cannonade begins in earnest and continues intermittently until 13 June.
4 June	Second battle at Windmill Hill. Jacobite attack repulsed. Colonel Butler, son of Lord Mountgarret, captured.
8 June	*Greyhound* near Culmore. Sailors report Jacobites building new boom across the river. Vessel badly damaged by fire from Culmore.
9 June	St Columba's Day. Firing ceases due to feast day.
11 June	Kirke arrives in Lough Foyle.
13 June	Firing stops. Defenders see Kirke's fleet in the lough.
15 June	HMS *Dartmouth* joins Kirke.
17 June	Near mutiny in the city as the soldiers loot food stores.
18 June	Attempts by garrison to contact Williamite forces at Enniskillen by boat lead to a skirmish on the river south of the city. City Market House demolished 'by the rabble'.
19 June	Council of War aboard the *Swallow* decides to await the arrival of more forces from Scotland before attempting offensive action.
20 June	General Rosen arrives from Dublin with reinforcements for the Jacobites. Rosen steps up operations to capture the city.
21 June	Firing begins again from the west of the city and continued sporadically for a month. During the last week of the siege, at the end of July, cannonballs and mortar rounds were continuously lobbed into the city. Governor Baker, grievously ill, recommends Colonel Mitchelburne as his replacement.
25 June	Captain Roche brings a communication from Kirke to the city.
26 June	Roche is wounded attemting to go back to the fleet and swims back across the Foyle to Derry. Another man drowned making the same attempt. On behalf of James I Colonel O'Neill parlays with Colonels Lance and Campbell to offer terms to the garrison. Offer refused.
28 June	Jacobite attack at Butcher Gate led by the earl of Clancarty repulsed with heavy loss.
30 June	Death of Governor Baker. Mitchelburne appointed in his place and released from confinement. End of June surrender

negotiations begin. Continue for some weeks. Breakdown of negotiations prompts new bombardment.

French envoy, D'Avaux, urges James to abandon the siege at Derry. Common knowledge that William intends to land an army in Ireland.

2 July — Kirke sends a regiment to Inch by sea to take the Jacobites in the rear. Nothing comes of this ploy.

2-3 July — General Rosen drives all the Protestants (around 1,200 men, women and children), within ten miles of the city before the city walls. Defenders retaliate by setting up a gallows on the Double Bastion and threaten to hang their prisoners.

4 July — Hostages before the walls allowed to return to their homes unmolested. The besiegers supplied them with food and money for their journey. Gallows removed from the bastion.

8 July — Garrison now reduced to 5,520.

10 July — Jacobites offer terms. Conveyed by means of firing a hollowed out bomb into the city. Defenders enter into negotiations.

13 July — Six commissioners from the city parlay with the besiegers. Cut short by promise from Kirke to attack the Jacobite forces from Inch island. Council of War debates the terms.

14 July — Council of War reassembles. Governor Walker in favour of surrender but overruled. Council adopts the policy of No Surrender if they were not given until 26 July to consider proposals. Negotiations end.

16 July — Kirke's fleet sails from Lough Foyle into Lough Swilly with the object of attacking from the rear. Skirmishing at Butcher Gate. Adam Murray badly wounded.

17 July — Desultory skirmishing continues.

18 July — A messenger from Kirke informs the defenders that he will shortly relieve them.

20 July — Jacobite forces reduced to about 5,000. Jacobite Council of War concludes the city cannot be taken by storm but must be starved out.

22 July — James reluctantly agrees to withdraw from Derry on the advice of his officers that it could not be taken by force. Messenger brings more news of Kirke to the city. He will attempt their relief within four days.

23 July — An attempted mutiny, with the object of surrendering the city on terms, is foiled by the arrest of the ringleaders. Since the previous week there have been courts martial held every day.

24 July	Council of War held in the city. Resolved to butcher all the cattle left in the city and to attempt the capture of others from the Jacobites.
25 July	Defenders attempt to seize Jacobite cattle at Pennyburn. Attack fails.
28 July	Breaking of the boom. City relieved.
1 August	Jacobite forces withdraw.
4 August	Kirke arrives in the city.
9 August	Governor Walker leaves for London.
13 August	Schomberg lands at Bangor with 20,000 men.
31 August	Jacobite forces routed by Williamites at Newtonbutler.
13 September	Governor Walker, in London, publishes *A True Account of the Siege of Londonderry*.

1690

March	7,000 French troops arrive under Marshal Lauzun. Mountcashel takes 5,000 Irish troops to France as compensation.
14 June	William of Orange lands at Carrickfergus.

Introduction:
the siege: myth and reality

T.G. Fraser

Sieges are the stuff of which legends are made. Homer and Virgil knew this when they wrote of the siege of Troy and the fate of its heroes. Victory in the ten-year siege gave the Greek city states their founding myths, while, as every schoolboy and schoolgirl once knew, the exiled Trojan Aeneas's landing on the Lavinian beaches resulted in the legendary foundation of Rome. In modern Ireland, similar legends have clustered around the siege of Derry, the longest and most celebrated of its kind in Irish or British history. Each year on the Saturday closest to 12 August, at 12:30 a.m. the branch clubs of the Apprentice Boys of Derry begin to march across Craigavon Bridge from their assembly points in the Waterside to enter the walled city, symbolically re-enacting the relief of the city in 1689. The Parent Clubs, based in the city, to which they are affiliated preserve the names associated with the siege. The Apprentice Boys of Derry Clubs honour the thirteen apprentices who closed the city gates in the face of the Earl of Antrim's soldiers in December 1688, the Walker, Mitchelburne and Baker Clubs are named after the three governors, the No Surrender Clubs echo the slogan of the city's defenders, the Browning Clubs commemorate the captain of the *Mountjoy* who was killed as his vessel broke the boom across the river Foyle, the Campsie Clubs represent one of the original apprentices, while at the rear of the procession march the Murray Clubs, their position acknowledging the rearguard actions of the siege's military hero, Colonel Adam Murray. Taking some two and a half hours to pass a given point, this is the largest Protestant procession in Northern Ireland, and probably one of the biggest popular demonstrations in contemporary Europe, even though, as Brian Walker shows in this book, this was by no means always the case.

The appeal of the siege traditions to a significant section of Protestant opinion is not in serious doubt, but in a society as divided as Northern Ireland there is inevitably another view of these events. Since 1995, the siege commemorations have taken on a sharp edge, with nationalist residents of the city contesting certain aspects of the day's events. What lay at the heart of the dispute was the morning circuit of the walls by the eight local Parent Clubs, a possibility re-opened in 1995 when the republican and loyalist ceasefires enabled the security forces to permit access to the circuit of the walls for the first time since 1969. When it became clear that the Apprentice Boys had applied for permission to parade the walls, a meeting in the Bogside denounced the proposed route as 'triumphalist'. What was at issue was the stretch of wall overlooking the nationalist Bogside. By the following year, the essential elements of the debate had come into focus. What for the Apprentice Boys was the maintenance of a tradition, for nationalists was conditional on their right of consent, summed up in the slogan painted on gable walls 'No consent. No parade'. Although couched in modern language, this was the reappearance of a recurring theme in the city's history, explored here by Mark McGovern, which dates back to the early nineteenth century.[1]

Historians are well aware of the processes by which in the course of the nineteenth century 'traditions' came to be created.[2] Every emergent nationalist movement found it necessary to validate itself by discovering a distinctive history and culture, and Irish political groups, whether nationalist or unionist, were no different. But, as William Kelly observes in his chapter, myths have ultimately to be grounded in some kind of reality. Despite the cold water dashed on the concept of a siege of Derry by the writer Hilaire Belloc and the historian Sir Charles Petrie, there is no reason to doubt the reality of what happened in 1688-9. Sieges are a peculiar form of warfare since they are generally the result of defeat or panic. A military force which is besieged has lost the initiative, since it has forfeited the ability to manoeuvre and has become dependent on a force coming to its relief. While its defences might give the appearance of security, the reality is that a beseiged force has become reliant upon a finite amount of food and military supplies. Even worse in the pre-modern period was the vulnerability of a water supply which could all too easily become polluted, with the inevitable consequence of epidemic disease.[3] The position of Derry exhibited all of these drawbacks, with the added vexation that its military leader Colonel Robert Lundy, believing it to be indefensible, had left it to its fate. George Walker's account, partial though it is in many respects, sums up the problems exactly:

> It did beget some disorder amongst us, and confusion, when we looked about us, and saw what we were doing; our Enemies all about us and our Friends running away from us; our Garrison we had compos'd of a number of poor people, frightened from their own homes, and seem'd more fit to hide themselves than to face an enemy; when we consider'd we had no Persons of any Experience in War amongst us, and those very

1 See Fraser, 'The Apprentice Boys and the Relief of Derry Parades', in Fraser (ed.), *The Irish Parading Tradition*. 2 For a seminal discussion, see E.J. Hobsbaum and T. Ranger, *The Invention of Tradition* (Cambridge, 1984). 3 There is a discussion of the problems of the besieged in William Seymour, *Great Sieges of History* (London, 1991), which includes a chapter 'Londonderry, 1689'.

Persons that were sent to assist us, had so little confidence in the Place, that they no sooner saw it, but they thought fit to leave it; that we had but a few Horse to Sally out with, and no Forage; no Engineers to Instruct us in our Works, no Fire-works, not so much as a Hand-Granado to annoy the enemy; not a Gun well mounted in the whole Town; that we had so many Mouths to feed, and not above ten days Provision for them.[4]

Walker's words could easily find their place in a military manual so well do they describe the plight of a beseiged force. To illustrate the problems of the beseiged we need look no further than the Second World War. The city of Leningrad endured a siege like no other. It began on 8 July 1941 and did not end until January 1944. Its successful defence rested on the hardiness of its defenders and the inability of the Germans to close the Soviet supply line across Lake Ladoga. Even so, by the end of its 900-day siege almost one million people had died. At Stalingrad the result was very different. On 23 November 1942, Colonel-General Friedrich Paulus's Sixth Army, some 250,000 men, was surrounded. Forbidden by Hitler to break out, Paulus's troops awaited relief by Field-Marshal von Manstein's Army Group Don. But Manstein, the ablest German commander of the war, could not effect relief, and on 31 January 1943 the remnants of the Sixth Army surrendered. Not even the greatest disaster in German military history could disuade Hitler from defending further besieged positions. From 26 December 1944 until 13 February 1945, Budapest became a second Stalingrad where once again a German army was annihilated in a vain attempt to defend the Hungarian oil-fields from the advancing Red Army. By its end much of what had been one of central Europe's most gracious cities lay in ashes. The Allies, too, had their siege misfortunes, the Americans with forlorn heroism at Corregidor in the Philippines, the British rather less creditably at Singapore where some 85,000 Imperial troops surrendered to 35,000 Japanese. In the post-war period the French debacle at Dien Bien Phu in 1954 confirmed the perils of siege warfare.

On balance, then, it might be said that subsequent historical experience suggests that the advantage rests with the besiegers rather than the besieged. Having said that, it is, of course, one of history's truisms that it is generally written by the victors, and this is certainly true of the siege of Derry. In a curious way we are well served by the polemics of the rival accounts of George Walker and John Mackenzie, analysed here by Jim Smyth. Not only do they expose the simmering tensions between episcopalian and presbyterian but in the course of doing so they round out our understanding of the Williamite side

4 George Walker, *A True Account of the Siege of London-Derry*, edited by Rev. P. Dwyer 1893, republished Wakefield, 1971, p. 20.

of the siege. It is, for example, to Mackenzie that we must turn for an account of Adam Murray's critical, perhaps even decisive, role in events, since he barely appears in Walker's account.[5] Walker and Mackenzie, both writing for the public, are usefully supplemented by the diary of Captain Thomas Ash, Dr Aiken's poem 'Londeriados', and *Ireland preserv'd: or, the siege of Londonderry*, a play written by siege governor John Mitchelbourne. The Jacobite side of the siege is by comparison opaque.

Mitchelburne, a curiously elusive character in the Walker and Mackenzie narratives, is nevertheless a key figure in understanding how the traditions of the siege came to be nurtured. The ideas of siege in the eighteenth century, explored by Breandán MacSuibhne and Robert Welch, owe much to Mitchelburne's determination that these events, in which his family had died of disease, should be commemorated. From records which seem once to have existed in the city, it is possible that in 1714, the twenty-fifth anniversary of the siege, he formed a club of Apprentice Boys. Dying in 1721, he left money in his will to ensure that the crimson flag which had indicated the state of siege would be flown from the cathedral.[6] The historical trail, already somewhat tenuous, then deserts us for much of the eighteenth century, but since 1759 a parade was held in the city to celebrate the Battle of Boyne it is probable that the siege was also marked in some way.[7] By the 1770s, it is clear that the siege of 1688-1689 had entered into the city's collective memory in a way in which, as William Kelly explains, its predecessor of 1649 had not. The centenary commemorations in 1788-1789 were events of some note, with, as is often emphasised, the participation of both bishops, the Earl of Bristol and Dr McDevitt, as well as the anonymous 'Presbyterian Ministers, and Elders'. Part of the celebration included the re-erection of Bishop's Gate as a memorial arch to King William III, though a statue of the king which was to have been crowned it never materialised. The event was remembered as one in which 'all sectarian and political differences were happily laid aside, in the universal rejoicing for the triumph of that civil and religious liberty, a blessing to all, which was celebrated on this occasion'.[8]

As this book explains, such apparent harmony dissolved rapidly in the early nineteenth century, since the passions of Irish politics quickly found their local expression. The most obvious symbol of this was the elevation of Walker to mythic status. The laying of the foundation stone of his memorial pillar in

5 For a discussion of the Walker-Mackenzie debate, see I. McBride, *The Siege of Derry in Ulster Protestant Mythology* (Dublin, 1997).   6 R.M. Sibbett in *Orangeism in Ireland and throughout the empire* (London, 1938), pp. 190-1, refers to an account supplied by Benjamin J. Darcus detailing the members of the club Mitchelburne formed in 1714.   7 See James Kelly, 'The Emergence of Political Parading, 1660-1800', in Fraser (ed.) *The Irish Parading Tradition*.   8 Colonel Colby, *Ordnance Survey of the county of Londonderry* (Dublin, 1837, reprinted with an introduction by Tony Crowe, Limavady, 1990), p. 49.

1826 followed the ending of military participation in the siege commemorations two year before. Any continuation of the siege traditions now fell on popular initiative. The erection of the pillar was one sign of this. With its statue of Walker beckoning towards the relieving fleet, the pillar represented the spirit of Protestant defiance. By 1832, the effigy of Lundy was being burned from the pillar, establishing a tradition which became part of the commemorations. But dominating as it did the rapidly growing Catholic area of the Bogside, it also became the focus of resentment. In time, the Bogsiders established their own tradition, of setting their chimneys on fire and relying on the west wind to blow the smoke on the Apprentice Boys assembling on the stretch of wall around the pillar. In August 1973, the pillar was blown up.

Brian Walker has traced the growth in the Apprentice Boys clubs in the 1840s and 1850s. What made their commemorations increasingly problematic was that they were taking place in a city undergoing a fundamental demographic change as Catholics settled in increasing numbers from rural Donegal. Although the city's symbols were Protestant, by the mid century Catholics were in a clear majority. For them, the traditions of the siege were but the uncomfortable reminder of the era of the Penal Laws and of subjection. But as Jim Smyth reminds us in his chapter, Presbyterians, too, were disadvantaged in the decades after the siege. Such tensions within the Protestant community continued to find an echo well into the nineteenth century. They can be seen in the rancorous aftermath of the 1868 election in the city when the Liberal Richard Dowse, himself an Episcopalian but supported by Catholics and members of the Presbyterian elite, defeated the Episcopalian Conservative Lord Claude Hamilton, the favoured candidate of the Apprentice Boys and their Governor, John Guy Ferguson. Although the picture is complicated by the fact that although Hamilton actually had a majority amongst Presbyterian voters in the election, Dowse still polled sufficiently well amongst Presbyterians to win him the seat.[9]

The tensions generated by the election found their focus the following April when Price Arthur, the Queen's son, visited the city. Three people were shot dead in clashes between the Apprentice Boys and their opponents. The siege commemorations were to feature prominently in the subsequent committee of enquiry. Spokesmen for the Apprentice Boys vigorously defended their right to celebrate the siege, attributing the opposition to Catholics who had recently arrived in the city, while Catholic and Presbyterian witnesses advocated the suppression of the relief parades. The commission itself identified a clash of perception which could stand for 1869 and long after: 'while to heighten the difficulty of the case, the city of their common habitation is one, whose heroic defence, at the time of that civil conflict, is the proudest recollection of the one

9 See B.M. Walker, *Ulster Politics. The Formative Years 1868-86* (Belfast, 1989), pp 62-3.

section, while its celebration, for the other, is identified with the memory of not only the reverses and ruin which befell their side in the struggle, but with that of long-after days of bitter humiliation'.[10]

One hundred years later, that fault line in the city's population remained. In the intervening century, Episcipalians and Presbyterians had drawn together in their opposition to Home Rule, Northern Ireland had been established and in the course of the 1920s the siege of Derry had become incorporated into the fabric of state. The distinctive position of the city, with its substantial nationalist majority, within Northern Ireland is too well known to need repetition here. The Relief parade of 1969 proved to be the catalyst for a sequence of events which changed the politics of Northern Ireland. Echoing the words of its predecessor one hundred years before, the official committee of enquiry under Mr Justice Scarman, which investigated the 1969 disturbances, noted that as the parade 'with its bands and regalia moved through the streets, it evoked a sense of pride and triumph in Protestant hearts, but a feeling of irritation and frustration in some of the Catholics'.[11] As the Murray Clubs at the end of the procession passed through Waterloo Place, missiles were thrown at the police and marchers by nationalist youths. The subsequent 'Battle of the Bogside', and even more serious communal riots in Belfast, led to the deployment of the British army, at first in a peacekeeping and then in a security role. By 1972, especially after the events of 'Bloody Sunday' in the city, the British government had decided that devolved government in Northern Ireland had run its course. The suspension of the Northern Ireland government on 24 March 1972 led to a prolonged period of 'Direct Rule' from London and the search for a new form of political accommodation.

As the political situation in Northern Ireland lurched out of control, with the beginning of the campaigns by republican and loyalist paramilitaries, commemorating the siege almost disappeared. In 1970, faced with a ban on parades, there was a rally at St Columb's Park in the Waterside, while the following year, after the introduction of internment, only seventy-four people, including the clergy, attended a service in St Columb's Cathedral. In 1972, after the Association's General Committee had announced that only the cathedral service would take place, forty clubs and bands paraded in the Waterside.[12] In 1975, the main parade returned to the cityside. By then, the Protestant population of the city felt under considerable pressure. As violence intensified, thousands of Protestants left the west bank for the Waterside or moved from the city altogether. But these events did not mean that the legacies of the siege

---

10 *Report of commissioners of inquiry, 1869, into the riots and disturbances in the city of Londonderry* (Dublin, 1869), p. 15.   11 *Violence and civil disturbances in Northern Ireland in 1969* (Cmd. 566, Belfast, 1972), p. 68.   12 Fraser 'The Apprentice Boys and the Relief of Derry Parades', in Fraser (ed.), *The Irish parading tradition*.

had lost their appeal for the wider Protestant community, rather the contrary. After the lean years of the early 1970s, the relief processions returned in full vigour and the evidence suggests that the Apprentice Boys Association continued to expand. A particular area of recruitment was Scotland, which provides an interesting example of how the traditions of the siege took root outside Ulster. J.R. Young's chapter explains how the siege had important resonances in contemporary Scotland, but it cannot be argued that this interest was then sustained. Although there were Apprentice Boys clubs in Glasgow before the First World War, when a Glasgow and District Amalgamated Committee was set up in 1946 only three clubs affiliated to it. It was not until the late 1950s that a group of enthusiasts started branches of the Walker Club in Caldercruix and Irvine, and by the early 1960s that they were strong enough to hold their own annual parade. By the mid-1990s, some forty clubs were affiliated to the Scottish Amalgamated Committee, whose May demonstration was a major feature of the Scottish marching calendar. The General Committee of the Apprentice Boys has for some years been led by a Glasgow band at the relief celebrations as a siege of Derry commemoration.[13]

This book opens up new perspectives on the myths and traditions of the siege as they have adapted, and been perceived, over time. The late seventeenth century was an age of siege warfare in Europe and that of Derry was far from being the most significant. The siege of Vienna in 1683 turned back the final thrust of Islam into central Europe, setting the scene for the Habsburg conquest of much of the continent. The Vienna of the baroque, the city that heard the glories of Haydn, Mozart and Beethoven, can be traced to that event. But who today commemorates the siege of Vienna? No one who has been in Derry for the annual parades in August and December can be in any doubt of the fact that for many people tradition, myth and conflict continue to reflect contemporary loyalties, anxieties and hopes, tenaciously so.

The issues discussed in this Introduction have been explored in 'The siege: its history and legacy, 1688-1889' in Gerard O'Brien (ed.), *Derry and Londonderry. History and Society* (Dublin, 1999); 'The Apprentic Boys and the Relief of Derry Parades', in T.G. Fraser (ed.), *The Irish Parading Tradition. Following the Drum* (Basingstoke, 2000); and a paper 'Commemorating the siege of Londonderry: tradition and conflict' presented to the conference 'Cities under siege/Sizuazione d'Assedio' held under the auspices of University of Siena in 1999 and which will appear in a volume of the same name. Crown Copyright material is reproduced by the permission of the Controller of Her Majesty's Stationery Office.

---

13 See account by William Gray 'A Short History of The Scottish Amalgamated Committee of The Apprentice Boys of Derry' in *Official brochure of the tercentenary celebrations of the Apprentice Boys of Derry Association* (Londonderry, 1988).

Siege, myth and history: Derry 1688-1998

Jim Smyth

The siege of Derry, which lasted from December 1688 to August 1689, generated one of the most enduring and resonant popular 'myths' of Irish history.[1]
With its elements of treachery and betrayal, courage, suffering, and triumph
against the odds, it stands as the archetype of what is sometimes called the
'siege metaphor', or more commonly the 'siege mentality', of the Ulster loyalist community. To loyalists in our own time the past is not another country. On
the contrary, as the Unionist politician, Peter Robinson, wrote of the siege, 'the
parallels to the present day are plain', or as the Apprentice Boy, Derek Miller,
observed in his evocatively titled pamphlet, *Still under Siege*, 'one of the virtues
of history is that it teaches us who we are and why . . . the Ulster Protestant
will still remain steadfast to his birthright and the biblical faith which he holds
dear'.[2] Such incorrigible present-mindedness is, of course, the worst of here-
sies against the canons of an historical revisionism long predicated upon a
philosophically limp opposition of 'fact' – 'what actually happened' – to
'myth'. Scholars of that persuasion draw a correlative distinction between
archive-based, intellectually detatched, 'professional' history, on the one hand,
and inadequately sourced, ideologically contaminated 'popular' history, on the
other. Accordingly popular myths, or narratives, are more likely to be viewed
as politically-charged misrepresentations of the past, to be debunked, dis-
pelled, or exploded, by a 'scientific' prospecting of the hard evidence, than as
important historical phenomena worthy of investigation in their own right.[3]

The empirical question: 'What actually happened'? demands an answer,
even if it can never be answered definitively. But so too do the questions: why,
and how, did 'what actually happened' come to be remembered in particular
ways? Why are other things which 'actually happened', forgotten (or silenced)?

1 Since the original version of this essay was presented as a paper to a conference on the siege at
Derry in 1995, the first full scholarly treatment of the subject has appeared with Ian McBride's
The siege of Derry in Ulster Protestant mythology (Dublin, 1997). 2 P. Robinson, *Their cry was
'No Surrender': an account of the siege of Londonderry 1688-9* (Belfast, 1988), p. 19; Derek Miller,
Still under siege (Lurgan, 1989), p. 58. 3 The literature on 'mythology' and revisionism in Irish
history has been growing steadily in recent years, much of it anthologized in C. Brady (ed.),
Interpreting Irish history (Dublin, 1994). The most succinct exposition of the classic anti-myth
position is T.W. Moody, 'Irish History and Irish Mythology', reprinted in Brady, pp 71-86.

Moreover, such understandings of the past, shared, as Joep Leersson points out, by 'generations of reasonably sane and reasonably well-informed people', acted as an 'operative force in historical development'.[4] These questions raise issues about what has been called 'social memory', or to use the French historian, Pierre Nora's concept, *lieux de memoire* ('sites of memory') which have increasingly engaged the attention of British, American, French, and indeed Irish historians.[5] The centrality of myth and remembrance in Irish politics and society is demonstrated by the rituals and iconography of commemoration; by parades, bonfires, statues and wall murals, often accompanied by specific injunctions to 'Remember 1690', 1916 or 1969. Thus the widely-held assumption that there exists a uniquely Irish blend – baleful, intense and divisive – of 'history' and politics. In Ireland 'History' is contested. William Cobbett once advised that there would be no peace on the streets of Dublin until the statue of William III in College Green was removed.[6] Like so many other Irish *lieux de memoire*, including the Walker momument erected to commemorate the siege of Derry, it was eventually blown up.

But the 'myths we live by' are not necessarily contentious or, as some Irish historians suppose, harmful. Nor are they as 'plain' and unchanging as their adherents believe. There has, for example, always been a variety of sieges of Derry from which to choose. If, as A.T.Q. Stewart suggests, the defence of Derry 'provides the paradigm for the entire history of the siege of the plantation',[7] it also serves as a paradigm for Presbyterian-Episcopalian rivalry. In his biography *Dissenter and Blackmouth*, the Presbyterian minister and historian, J.M. Barclay, recalls growing up in that city as a teenager in the 1920's: 'I walked the walls. I read McKenzie's *Siege of Derry*, and saw Walker's account for what it was.'[8] The dismissal is as brisk as it is absolute. The Revd George Walker's celebrated history of the siege deserved no further comment. Barclay might have elaborated, however, because he touches here on an originary moment in the disputed legacy of the siege. Certainly in the years immediately after 1689 Governor Walker's account, John McKenzie's reply, and Walker's further *Vindication*, came to symbolize the bitter rivalries between presbyterians and the established church, as much as the siege itself was claimed by others to symbolize pan-protestant solidarity.

In retrospect Walker lacks credibility as a reliable witness. He wrote as a

4 J. Leerssen, *Remembrance and imagination: patterns in the historical and literary representations of Ireland in the nineteenth century* (Cork, 1997).   5 P. Norra, *Realms of memory, vol. 1: conflicts and divisions* (New York, 1992); P.H. Hutton, *History as an art of memory* (London, 1993); R. Samuel, *Theatres of memory* (London, 1994); for a summary of these historiographical developments see the chapter 'History as social memory' in P. Burke, *Varieties of cultural history* (Ithaca, NY, 1997). 6 M. Craig, *Dublin, 1660-1860* (Dublin, 1980 ed.), p. 77.   7 A.T.Q. Stewart, *The narrow ground: the roots of conflict in Ulster* (London, 1989 ed.), p. 52.   8 J.M. Barkley, *Dissenter and blackmouth* (Belfast, 1991), p. 35.

churchman and an enemy of dissent. But at the time he enjoyed a great deal of credibility. A couple of days after the relief of the city he set out for London by way of Scotland. En route, he was made a free man of the city of Edinburgh, and awarded honorary doctorates by Oxford and Cambridge universities. Received at court he had his portrait commissioned by King William. The acclamation of the author bestowed kudos and authority upon his book. McKenzie, a Presbyterian minister from Cookstown who took refuge behind the walls, wrote a reply entitled: *A Narrative on the Siege of Londonderry: Or the late memorable transactions of that City. Faithfully represented to rectifie the mistakes, and supply the omissions of Mr Walker's account.* The dispute boiled down to names. Walker identified eighteen Church of Ireland ministers who were in the siege, but when he turned to the non-conforming ministers, his memory deserted him. He could recollect only seven, four of whom died during the ordeal, and all of whom remained nameless. This was dishonest, discourteous, and offensive. Indeed after McKenzie's riposte Walker published a further pamphlet, *A Vindication of the Account of the Siege of Derry*, in which he recovered his memory, but contrived to heep yet more insult upon injury by misspelling some of the non-conforming ministers names. Most notoriously, one of their number, Gilchrist, surfaced in the 'corrected' account as KiL-Christ![9]

The animosity provoked by this controversy was not soon forgotten. Barclay's aside appeared in a book published in 1991 and in the nineteenth century, another Presbyterian historian, Thomas Witherow, attacked Walker's version of events. In a little pamphlet, published in 1905, *The Roots of Presbyterianism in Donegal*, the Revd Alexander Lecky commends McKenzie's book as the best account available, and asserts that: 'the bulk of the men who took part in this memorable achievement [of defying the Jacobite forces] were of the Presbyterian faith – attempts have been made' he continued darkly, 'to show that they were not'. Lecky then cites near contemporary estimates which put the figures at sixteen or ten Presbyterians within the walls to every member of the established church.[10] It is true that a pan-Protestant interpretation of the siege achieved ascendancy from the nineteenth century, as Presbyterians and churchmen once more closed ranks in the face of the common Catholic enemy. There were no Presbyterian objections, for instance, to the erection of the Walker monument. Yet as recently as 1989, Gordon Lucy in his volume of extracts from Macauley's writings on 1688-90 in Ireland, *Macauley on Londonderry, Enniskillen and the Boyne*, adopts a distinctly presbyterian bias. Lucy links the passages from Macauley with his own editorialising, and concludes by

9 For an account of the post-seige debate see McBride, *The siege of Derry*, pp 27-32 and for Walker's reception in Britain, P. Macory, *The siege of Derry* (Oxford, 1988), p. 326. 10 A. Lecky, *The roots of Presbyterianism in Donegal* (Belfast, 1905), pp 24-5.

alluding to the post-siege discrimination experienced by dissenters well into the eighteenth century, and by celebrating the contribution of the Presbyterians – the Ulster Scots or 'Scotch- Irish' as they were known in America – to the American revolution. As the nineteenth-century historian, J.A. Froude, pointed out, many of those who fought on the American side – 'England's fiercest enemies' – were the grandsons and the great grandsons of the men who had defended the city of Derry in 1689. To Lucy the lessons of history are obvious: modern Ulster men can look with pride to the determination and the sheer love of liberty displayed by their gallant ancestors.[11]

Presbyterian narratives of the siege were almost pre-programmed by a rhetoric and imagery which the Ulstermen shared with their late seventeenth-century Scottish Covenanting kin. Presbyterian self images combined qualities of rectitude, staunchness, steadfastness, and integrity. The siege thus offered an examplar of that staunchness in the face of the greatest threat. Episcopalians in contrast were 'backsliders', and, fortunately for the Ulster-Scot world-view, a number of prominent churchmen obligingly played out their allotted role. The siege began when, in defiance of Bishop Hopkin's injunction to the townspeople and refugees to surrender to their lawful sovereign, the Apprentice Boys shut the gates. Governor Walker with his self-serving lies, and, of course, that great emblematic traitor of Ulster Protestant tradition, Colonel Lundy, were both Episcopalian.

Inter-protestant rivalries were certainly very evident in Derry city in the ten to fifteen years after the siege. In the 1690s Presbyterianism in Ulster experienced a new confidence and buoyancy. Before then, but particularly between 1660 and 1690, as the largest nonconforming sect outside the established church the Presbyterians were subject to civil disabilities. The revolution changed all that. The first dissenting synod in the British Isles was held in Ulster in 1690 and Presbyterianism became the established religion in Scotland the same year. Coming from the Dutch Calvinist tradition, William was less suspicious of Presbyterians than his Stuart predecessors, and in fact rewarded their services to the revolution by doubling the royal stipend, the *regium donum*, to Presbyterian ministers.

In addition to this new found security and status presbyterian numbers were boosted dramatically during the mid-1690s, when the collapse of the rural economy in Scotland caused a huge spurt of migration from the lowlands into Ulster. It has been estimated that in the decade following 1694 up to 60,000 Presbyterians fled from Scotland into the north of Ireland, many of whom settled in County Derry.[12] By 1700, Presbyterians probably outnumered

11 G. Lucy (ed.), *Macauley on Londonderry, Enniskillen and the Boyne* (Tandragee, 1989), p. 89.
12 [Sir Francis Brewster], *A discourse concerning Ireland and the different interests thereof* ... (London, 1698), pp 24-5, 28, 33-4

Episcopalians in Ulster. The new demographic balance worried the established church. Had the growth in the presbyterian population peaked, or would this dangerous trend continue? Nor can Episcopalian anxieties be overemphasised.[13] Presbyterians were viewed, inaccurately, as regicides, republicans and disciples of John Milton.[14] Just as dammingly they were accused of being Scots! They were were not to be trusted. The fears aroused within the episcopalian establishment by the Scottish influx of the 1690s, were voiced most forcefully by the new bishop of Derry, William King. During this period King engaged the dissenters, particularly the Presbyterians, in theological controversy. The timing and political context were crucial however. Presbyterian consolidation in Scotland and expansionism in Ulster, very visibily so in King's own jurisdiction of the diocese of Derry, all indicated a triumphant and, for the Established church, potentially diasterous, advance. The bishop complained about the clannishness of the Ulster Scots, and of their tendency to trade among themselves to the exclusion of their fellow Protestants. His hostility to presbyterianism, rooted in theology and his views of church government, was nourished by fear. To King, and to other churchmen, the Presbyterians posed a unique threat among the non-conformists. They were cohesive, concentrated, well-organized, expanding, and thought of themselves of belonging not to a mere sect, but to the true church.

If William secured his place in the 'glorious and immortal memory' of presbyterian Ulster, his successor, Anne, left a bitter aftertaste. A High Church partisan, harbouring a deep distrust of dissent, towards the end of her reign Anne actually suspended the *regium donum*. In 1704 the Act to Prevent the Further Growth of Popery was returned from England with a 'sacramental test' tacked onto it, obliging all public office holders to take the sacrament according to the rites of the established church. Since no Presbyterian could in good conscience do that, the test effectively proscribed them as well as Catholics from positions of trust under the crown – an irony seized by Daniel Defoe in his pamphlet: *The Parallel, or Persecution of Protestant Dissenters is the Best Way to Prevent the Growth of Popery in Ireland*. Notoriously the implementation of the sacramental test led to the purge of Derry corporation. A mere fifteen years after the siege, twenty-four of the corporation's thirty-eight members 'resigned', rather than take the test. The impact of this episode echoed down the decades. Presbyterians argued that as the people who had shut the gates against James and saved the revolution such discrimination was scant reward. As late as the 1790s Anne's reign was invoked as an era of

---

13 L.M. Cullen, *The emergence of modern Ireland, 1600-1900* (London, 1981), pp 12, 34, 39.
14 W. Tisdell, *The conduct of the dissenters of Ireland, with respect to both Church and State* (Dublin, 1712), p. 68. In view of Milton's bitter attack on the Belfast Presbytery in 1649 Tisdell's claim is, of course, ludicrous.

oppression in the Belfast United Irish newspaper, the *Northern Star.*[15] Similarly, the failure of the British government to honour its promise of compensation to siege survivors – recorded acidly in *A View of the Danger and Folly of Being Publick-Spirited, and Sincerely Loving One's Country* – entered the Presbyterian repertoire of grievance.

Many subsequent commentators have advanced large claims for the self evident significance of the siege in Irish history, British history and even European history. And there is a case to be made for its wider importance, but that is not necessarily how it would have appeared to someone in the eighteenth century. The siege, unlike the Boyne, or King William's birthday, did not figure as a national commemoration. It was, it is true, memorialized by one of the two great tapestries hung in the chamber of the House of Lords – the other depicted William crossing the Boyne – but otherwise commemorations were confined to Derry. A possible explanation for the comparative absence of national observance is that the contested aspects of the siege were troubling to the church interest, and therefore to the political elite in eighteenth-century Ireland.

Two more important dates in the eighteenth-century Irish Protestant calendar than either 12 December or 1 August, were 23 October, which marked the beginning of the 1641 massacres, and 4 November, the anniversary of William III's birthday. Sixteen forty-one was commemorated each year by Church of Ireland services.[16] Members of parliament, lords and commons, attended a service at Christ Church Cathedral, to hear a sermon preached by the parliamentary chaplain on the deliverance of the Protestant nation. Each 4 November ceremonies were held at the statue of William, commissioned by Dublin corporation in 1700, and erected in College Green in 1701. Significantly, these were official, government-sponsored, gatherings. Representing the 'authorized version' of the Williamite legacy, they were designed to underwrite and celebrate the protestant state which had emerged by 1691.[17]

In the late eighteenth century the emphasis, in terms both of who participated in commemoration, and of the interpretation of events, began to shift; the orientation became more ecumenical, non-sectarian and whiggish. This was the context for the remarkable festivities in Derry in 1788. The primary impetus to the new inclusiveness came from Volunteering. Catholics, many of whom supported, and some of whom would later join, the Volunteer movement, participated in the Volunteer commemoration of the Boyne, in

15 *Northern Star*, 22 Sep. 1792. **16** T.C. Barnard, 'The uses of the 23 Oct. 1641 and Irish Protestant celebrations', *English Historical Review 106* (1991), pp 889-920. **17** J.G. Simms, 'Remembering 1690', *Studies* 68 (1974), pp 231-42; J. Kelly, ' "The Glorious and Immortal Memory": Commemoration and Protestant identity in Ireland 1660-1800', *Proceedings of the Royal Irish Academy* 94c (1994), pp 25-52.

Drogheda, on 12 July 1780.[18] A new perspective on the events of the seventeenth century began to open up. In the late 1680s and 1690s to be an Irish Catholic was to be a Jacobite. For many Catholics in the first half of next century the equation held. By 1786, however, the founder of the Catholic Association, Charles O'Conor, felt able to write that 'we are all become *good Protestants in Politics*.'[19] He referred to the demise of Jacobitism, even as an aspiration, and to the 'enlightened' Catholic's embrace of whig 'revolution principles'. Catholics, if one accepts O'Connor's assertion, could now look to 1688-9 as a triumph of 'freedom, religion and laws' over popery and arbitrary power. 'Popery', after all, generally denoted a rebarbative *political* complex, standing for the antithesis of 'Liberty'. As Daniel O'Connell later put it, 'I am sincerely a Catholic, but not a papist'.[20]

The centenary celebrations in Derry had a Volunteering background. The earl bishop of Derry, Frederick Augustus Hervey, had been a vocal advocate, in Volunteer debates, of Catholic relief, and as part of the festivities in 1788 a poem was read praising him as 'a friend and benefactor of mankind'.[21] The celebrations were viewed as a notable public event at the time and are recorded in some detail. At dawn to the beat of drums, the ringing of bells, and the discharge of cannon, the aldermen and burgesses of the corporation dressed in full regalia, assembled with clergymen of all denominations, volunteers, the 'principal citizens' and apprentices, before processing to the cathedral and to the meeting house. HMS *Porcupine* anchored in the Foyle then fired off a 21-gun salute. Lundy's effigy was consigned once again to flames by 'the rabble', followed once again by the ritual closing of the gates. Finally, the city notables, including a number of Catholic priests, sat down to a 'plain but plentiful dinner' at the town hall.

The account above is lifted from John Graham's *History of the Siege of Derry and Defence of Enniskillen*, first published in 1823, and reprinted in 1829. Graham's gloss on these events is revealing. On the ecumenical and whiggish character of the celebration, he observed that 'no man was idiot enough to object to drink to the glorious memory of that great Prince who saved the religion of the Protestant, and the liberty of all other professors of Christianity ... Religious dissensions in particular seemed to be buried in oblivion as Roman Catholics vied with Protestants in expressing every possible mark of the sense of the blessings secured to them by the event which they were commemorating.' But then he goes on to lament how all this contrasted strongly with the brutal ignorance of the agitators of the present day. The

18 Simms, 'Remembering 1690', p. 234.   19 Charles O'Conor to Joseph C. Walker, 31 Jan. 1786 in C. Coogan Ward & R.E. Ward (eds), *The letters of Charles O'Conor of Belanagare*, vol. 2 (Ann Arbor, 1980), pp 236-7.   20 Quoted in D. Bowen, *The Protestant crusade in Ireland, 1800-70* (Dublin, 1978), p. 6.   21 W.S. Childe-Pemberton, *The earl-bishop. The life of Frederick Hervey, bishop of Derry, earl of Bristol* (London, 1924), vol. 2, p. 409.

'agitators' of O'Connell's movement for Catholic emancipation considered the honours paid to William's memory an insult to their religion.[22] What had happened between 1788 and 1829?

The short answer is the 1790s. Although the whig cult of William and non-sectarian character of the Derry centenary can be interpreted as evidence of the advance of 'enlightenment' and of religious tolerance among Protestants, the point should not be stretched too far. As the bloody sectarian conflict of the 1790s demonstrated, in Ireland lethal animosities were never far below the surface.[23] In the wake of the French Revolution both the movement for parliamentary reform and the Catholic Committee revived. This in turn provoked a fierce reaction, particularly against the campaign for Catholic relief. I have argued elsewhere that by 1792 people were afraid of a civil war breaking out; that the nation-wide mobilisation of the Catholic population was unprecedented; and that many in the protestant community were profoundly unnerved.[24] In response to the Catholic challenge, Dublin corporation issued a declaration of Protestant Ascendancy. Almost reflexively, at this moment of crisis, it invoked the struggle of the late seventeenth century, redefining, or retrieving, the legacy of 1688-91, in its sectarian colours:

> One hundred years are just elapsed, since the question was tried upon an appeal to heaven, whether this country should become a Popish kingdom, governed by an arbitrary and unconstitutional Popish tyrant . . . or enjoy the blessings of a free Protestant government . . . The great ruler of all things decided in favour of our ancestors . . . and Ireland became a Protestant nation enjoying a British constitution.

The Ascendancy thereby secured consisted of:

> A Protestant King of Ireland, a Protestant Parliament, a Protestant hierarchy, Protestant electors in government, the benches of justice, and the army and the revenue through all the branches and details Protestant;.and this system supported by a connection with the Protestant realm of England.[25]

22 J Graham, *A history of the siege of Derry and defence of Enniskillen in 1688 and 1689* (Dublin, 1829), pp 351-3.　**23** For a recent refutation of the theory that religious toleration was spreading in late eighteenth-century Ireland see I. McBride, '"When Ulster joined Ireland": Anti-popery, Presbyterian radicalism and Irish republicanism in the 1790s', *Past and present* 157 (1997), pp 63-93.　**24** J. Smyth, *The men of no property. Irish radicals and popular politics in the late eighteenth century* (London, 1992), pp 52-70.　**25** Quoted in W.E.H. Lecky, *A history of Ireland in the eighteenth century* (London, 1892), vol. 3, p. 64.

Three years later Protestant Ascendancy, thus defined, found new organizational expression in the Orange Order. At the outset a popular movement, founded by weavers, innkeepers and tailors, the Order was quickly commandeered by the protestant gentry. In the revolutionary 1790s the United Irishmen posed a major threat to government, and to the men of property.[26] Under such crisis conditions the British army generals stationed in Ireland and their political masters were forced into a reluctant alliance with a counter-revolutionary force too formidable to leave unharnessed. But the government remained uneasy in its relationship with Orangeism, partly because it did not exercise complete control over it, and partly because of it's potential for trouble and indiscipline. There was, and is, an ambivalence at the heart of Orangeism. On the one hand it champions civil and religious liberty, on the other it is explicitly sectarian. Alas, it was the militant sectarianism which ultimately overshadowed the more whiggish interpretation of the Williamite legacy.

Orangeism has always had a problem of respectability, the patronage of members of the royal family notwithstanding. During the eigthteenth century there existed a particular establishment version of the Williamite legacy, represented by the tapestries in the House of Lords and by the levies held at the Castle. By 1806, however, the Government had disengaged from celebrations of William's birthday, the Boyne and so on. Post-Union government developed a code of neutrality between 'factions'. The government no longer considered it it's business to support one version of Irish history, or one faction within Irish society and politics. Commemorations became an affair of (a faction of) the Protestant community, rather than, as hitherto, one of a Protestant government and a Protestant people. Indeed by 1822 Orange parades were banned outright.[27] And as the government opted out, liberal Protestants became openly critical of Orange demonstrations, which they regarded as divisive. In 1847 the familiarity of these condemnations can be felt behind the insistence of an apologist of the siege celebrations that they were intended 'merely to commemorate the triumph in that great event, and not, as some suppose, to glory over, or persecute an unoffending neighbour, who is of the adverse creed, by treating him with rancour, or personal violence'. Although a few paragraphs earlier the same author located the siege itself within an historic conflict between '*Jesuitism and Protestantism.*'[28]

In his essay, '1641, 1689, 1690 and all that – The Unionist Sense of History', Brian Walker notes that during July 1790, the centenary of the

26 J. Smyth, 'The men of no popery: the origins of the Orange Order', *History Ireland* 3/3 (1995).   27 J.R. Hill, 'National festivals, the State and "Protestant ascendancy"', *Irish Historical Studies* 24 (1984), pp 30-51.   28 R. Simpson, *The annals of Derry* (Derry, 1847; repr. Limavady, 1987), pp 181-2.

Boyne, the *Belfast Newsletter*, gives no account of any celebration to mark that event in the town.[29] Commemorations were held, however, in Drogheda, Downpatrick and Doagh. Belfast's silence is construed as evidence of discontinuity. Popular memory of Derry, the Boyne, and Aughrim, began to fade from the mid eighteenth century, before reviving in the late nineteenth century. It is suggestive, for instance, that nine of the twelve historical novels listed in Sam Burnside's bibliography of literary materials relating to the siege were published between 1877 and 1905.[30] The revival is attributed to the writings of Froude on 1641; to Macauley's classic account of the siege in his *History of England*; and to Thomas Witherow's very successful *Derry, Enniskillen – The Year 1689*, which was published in 1873. It is also attributed to the crisis which occurred in the 1880s, particularly 1886. That crisis, Walker believes, is the real smithy in which the new unionist sense of history was forged.

The thesis that a new unionist sense of history emerges at this moment fits neatly the time-frame adopted by Eric Hobsbawm in his introduction to The Invention of Tradition, 'Mass-Producing Traditions, Europe 1870-1914'.[31] If Hobsbawm is right, then Walker's historically-minded unionists conform to a European pattern. And yet the emphasis on the 1880s overlooks continuities. The almost annual 12 July riot in Belfast, inaugurated in 1813, remained a feature of Belfast street life throughout the nineteenth century.[32] Derry witnessed major riots in 1878 and 1879. A.T.Q Stewart advances the theory that rioting became much more serious in Derry because of the train.[33] Orange Men and Apprentice Boys were brought in from all over Ulster, and while it was one thing for local Apprentice Boys to taunt their neigbhours in the Bogside, it was quite another for outsiders from Newry or Enniskillen to do so!

Again, from the fiction of William Carleton it is clear that low level conflict between the Catholic Ribbonmen and their Orange rivals permeated rural Ulster for half a century and more before the 1880s. In Derry, the Apprentice Boys were founded in 1814, Graham's book appeared in 1823, and Walkers monument was erected in 1828. It should thus be possible to recognise that the 'myths' of 1688-90 achieved a new, more powerful, register in the Protestant imagination in the 1880s, without eliding their significance in that imagination before that decade.

Hobsbawm argues that all invented traditions are attempts to use imagined pasts to legitimate versions of the present and to reinforce group cohesion.

29 B. Walker, '1641, 1689, 1690 and all that – The Unionist sense of history', reprinted in Walker, *Dancing to history's tune: history, myth and politics in Ireland* (Belfast, 1996), pp 1-14. 30 S. Burnside, '"No temporising with the foe". Literary materials relating to the siege and relief of Derry', *Linen Hall Review* 5/3 (1988), pp 4-9. 31 E.J. Hobsbawm & T. Ranger (eds), *The invention of tradition* (Cambridge, 1984 ed.), pp 1-14. 32 Stewart, *The narrow ground*, pp 139-41. 33 Ibid., p. 73.

This is a conclusion he might have reached by reading the *Belfast Newsletter* of
1888. On Monday 13 August the *Newsletter* carried the following report:

> two great historical events will be commemorated today in
> Londonderry and in County Fermanagh and in other places ... the
> relief of the Maiden City ... loyal men think and speak of both in
> grateful remembrance. The city was held for Protestantism and the
> Prince and Princess of Orange. It is well to keep in mind the deeds of
> the past; to repair trophies; and to manifest a determination to uphold
> great principles. In the present, affairs indicate trouble, what Tyrconnell
> did openly Mr Gladstone is trying to do stealthily, and the unity of the
> Kingdom is threatened ... History is repeating itself; and patriotic sub-
> jects must be prepared to serve the rights of the crown and maintain the
> integrity of the constitution.

The next day it continued on these themes:

> Important as commemorations of this kind have been in the past, it is of
> even greater consequence that they should be kept up in the present ...
> and kept up with even greater determination and enthusiasm than ever.
> It may be said that Ireland is in almost as great a danger today as was the
> case when James II was aiming at the destruction of civil and religious
> liberty ... The danger is not any less but it is coming in a different way.

If James had succeeded the kingdom would have been 'completely at the
mercy of Rome'. If Gladstone succeeds, 'a nationalist parliament will be set up,
a parliament prepared to do the bidding of Rome, that will endeavour to crush
Protestantism and try to sever the remaining links binding Ireland to Great
Britain'.[34]

The rhetoric, and the assumptions about who it is that should be celebrating and what it is that they should be remembering, are illuminating. It is 'loyal
men' and 'Protestants', who are being summoned to the defence of the crown
and the British connection. The emphasis on Protestantism and loyalism is
narrow, exclusive, and, despite protestations to the contrary, sectarian. The
contrast with the centenary interpretation is complete.

The 1888 version of the siege has largely prevailed. With the establishment
of the Northern Ireland state in 1921 Orangeism entered into its institutional
heyday. During the Stormont era the Orange Order did not merely enjoy the
toleration or endorsement of the government; it actually infiltrated the apparatus of the state.[35] In that context commemorations of 'Derry, Enniskillen

34 *Belfast News Letter*, 13 & 14 Aug. 1888.   35 See the comments of Patrick Shea, *Voices and the*

and the Boyne' understood as a victory of Protestant and British values, once again received official sanction. Since 1925 the 12th of July has been a public holiday in Northern Ireland. A generous construction on the values celebrated on these occasions would stress 'civil and religious liberty', although 'triumphalism' is the word used most readily by northern Catholics to describe Orange and Apprentice Boy parades. The events at Drumcree and Derry in the 1990s appear to underline the belief that the impact of myth in a divided society is 'destructive', even 'lethal', and that rather than 'crippl[ing] ourselves unnecessarily with additional burdens from the past [which] make our difficulties all the greater', 'the myths of history must not be allowed to unduly affect peoples' minds and influence their judgement'. Rather one of the roles of the historian, according to this position, is to 'deflate epics' and to 'liberate' the community from 'servitude to the myth'.[36]

These commendable aspirations are not as straightforward as they may at first appear. Firstly, they proceed from an attitude which is *engage* and essentially political; that is they proceed from precisely the attitude which historians of the myth-debunking tendency decry. In an affectionate tribute to the eighteenth century historian, Maureen Wall, Tom Dunne recalls approvingly the following admonishment to University College Dublin undergraduates: 'You probably think that this is a dreadful country, and in many ways it is. But it's up to you *to do something about it* – don't walk away from it, stay here and *help to change it*.'[37] – Karl Marx, famously, held similar views about the proper function of intellectuals. Secondly, the sometimes explicit, sometimes implicit, alternative to 'myth' offered by such historians, namely the rigorous examination of archival evidence, often conceals an overestimate of the epistemological status of empirical enquiry, and an underestimate of the inexpungable rhetorical, fictive and ideological elements involved in the selection, organisation and presentation of data. A swingeing critique of the delusions of dispassionate 'objectivity' comes from a rather surprising quarter: a former student of T.W. Moody, Conor Cruise O'Brien. 'With Michelet and Carlyle,' writes O'Brien, 'the war was in the open country. Among modern scientific historians it is siege warfare, unrelenting hostilities, masked by long periods of apparent quiet. Then through the ideological slit windows in the massive fortifications of fact comes the crossbow bolt to transfix German, or Jew, or Jesuit.'[38]

sound of drums. An Irish autobiography (Belfast, 1981), pp 161-2, 198. See also G.S. Walker, *The politics of frustration. Harry Midgley and the failure of labour in Northern Ireland* (Manchester, 1985), pp 181-2. **36** B.M. Walker, *Dancing to history's tune*, pp 74, 158; R.F. Foster, 'The problems of writing Irish history', *History Today* 34 (1984), p. 30; T.W. Moody, 'Irish history and Irish mythology', p. 86. **37** T. Dunne, 'Maureen Wall (nèe McGeehin) 1918-1972: a memoir' in G. O'Brien (ed.), *Catholic Ireland in the eighteenth century: collected essays of Maureen Wall* (Dublin, 1989), pp 5-6. Italics added. **38** C.C. O'Brien, 'Michelet today' in *Writers and politics.Eessays and criticism* (London, 1965), p. 76.

Perhaps it is time for revisionist historians to follow O'Brien's example, and to direct the same scepticism which they apply to their sources, and to myth, towards their own craft.

Finally, as the centenary celebrations of the siege of Derry demonstrated, even in divided societies one man's myth need not inevitably open another man's wounds. Collective myths – which are in any event inescapable – have a protean quality, and can bind communities in positive ways. Sloganizing about 'civil and religious liberty' may sound as hollow to the residents of Derry's Bogside or Portadown's Garvaghy Road as the ritual invocation of 'freedom' and 'equality' does to African Americans, yet as the American historian, William H. McNeill has argued, 'Myths are, after all, often self-validating . . . What is can move toward what ought to be, given commitment to a flattering self-image. The American civil rights movement of the fifties and sixties illustrates this phenomenon amongst us.'[39] The fecund complexities and multiple meanings of 'popular mythology' require careful scrutiny; not simply as reality-distorting anti-history, but as a vital dimension, creative as well as destructive, to the historical process itself.

39 W.H. McNeill, 'Mythistory, or truth, myth, history, and historians', *American Historical Review* 91/1 (1986), p. 6.

The forgotten siege of Derry, March-August, 1649

W.P. Kelly

At one point in their mile long circumference the seventeenth-century walls of Derry loom some hundreds of feet above the Bogside. A nationalist area of the city, the Bogside is viewed by the media, the security forces and anyone who knows anything at all about the 'Troubles,' as a hotbed of Irish Republican activity. The Unionist Apprentice Boys of Derry, whose headquarters adjoin the walls here, enjoy pointing out to visitors that the cannons menacing the Bogside at this point are in fact republican cannons.[1] They are republican because they were sent by the London Companies to assist the parliamentarian officer Sir Charles Coote, besieged in Derry by the combined forces of royalism in Ulster after the execution of Charles I in January 1649.[2]

The purpose of this essay is to give some account of how and why these cannons came to be in Londonderry. But it is not merely an historical account. In pointing up the apparent contradiction, in terms of present day politics of the city, of 'republicans' menacing 'Republicans' the Apprentice Boys unwittingly put their finger on the tortured nature of both seventeenth- and twentieth-century politics of Derry, Ireland and in Britain. What actually saved the day for Sir Charles at Derry, and for the parliament in England, was not extra cannon but the intervention of that great icon of Irish nationalist tradition, Owen Roe O'Neill, commander of an overwhelmingly Gaelic Irish and Catholic army in Ulster.[3]

But, although these were important events in the history of these islands, this siege is largely forgotten. A.T.Q. Stewart has remarked that 'significantly [1649] has not entered into the mythology of either Catholic or Protestant.[4]

---

1 The Apprentice Boys of Derry were founded to commemorate the action of thirteen young men who, in defiance of the city fathers and in direct disobedience to the orders of the lord lieutenant of Ireland, slammed the gates of the city against the advancing troops of the Earl of Antrim in December 1688. This action, and the seizure of the magazine shortly after, led eventually to the Siege of Derry in the following year when James II attempted to retake the city. 2 England became a republic when monarchy was abolished in May 1649. See Thomas Carte: 'Coote . . . reduced all Ulster under the power of the "parliamentarian or republican army,"' cited in R. Simpson, *The annals of Derry*, reprint (Limavady, 1987), p. 75. 3 Edward, Hyde, earl of Clarendon, *The history of the rebellion and civil war in Ireland* (Dublin, 1719-20), p. 82. 4 A.T.Q.,

The siege is either dismissed in a few lines or not mentioned at all. It is hardly surprising therefore that it is still a shock to many to discover that the city was besieged on more than one occasion.[5] Sieges other than 1689, the settlement was sacked in 1608 and briefly invested in 1641, are not commemorated in any way in the city or elsewhere. Indeed, the other essays in this present volume highlight the contrast between two sets of events: 1689 is remembered, commemorated, researched, and has been the subject of innumerable books, articles and pamphlets.[6] For 1649 there is a scant historiography. The events of 1689 on the other hand are, some would say, commemorated *ad nauseam* and annual celebrations of these events are even today a contentious issue in the city. This paper will argue that there are reasons why 1649 is largely forgotten. Sections one and two of this essay will provide a short contextual account of the events leading to the siege of 1649. The following section will briefly rehearse the siege itself. Finally, section four will explore in greater depth why these events are not commemorated to the same degree as 1689.

I

It is no overstatement to say that most historians of this period preface their arguments with the caveat that the situation in Ireland in 1649 was 'very complex'. Perhaps a clue to this complexity lies in the designation of these events by historians as 'The War(s) of the Three Kingdoms', or the 'British Civil Wars'.[7] The nature of the triple monarchy, Charles I was king of Ireland, Scotland and England, ensured that events in one kingdom had consequences in the others. In 1638 the largely Calvinist Scots rejected the king's religious reforms and went to war to defend their position. The humiliation of the king gave the Irish, the Gaelic Irish of Ulster in particular, the opportunity to overthrow the plantation.[8] Events were complicated even further in August 1642 when the crisis between the king and the English parliament broke out into civil war. In Ireland therefore at least four combatant forces emerged. Soon

Stewart, *The narrow ground, aspects of Ulster, 1609-1969* (London, 1977), p 61.   **5** For instance, see P.R. Newman, *Companion to Irish history from the submission of Tyrone to partition, 1603-1921* (Oxford, 1991), p 48; the most widely cited history of the walls of Derry by Milligan refers to 1649 in only a few lines; Jonathan Bardon's *History of Ulster*, discusses events in Ulster after the siege but not the siege itself, pp 140-1; J.S. Reid, the historian of the Presbyterian church, suggests that the siege of 1649 is forgotten because it 'eclipsed by the second [1689]': J.S. Reid, *History of the Presbyterian church in Ireland*, vol. 2 (2 ed., London, 1853), p. 104.   **6** See Bibliography.   **7** J. Morrill, 'Historical Introduction and Overview: The Un-English Civil War,' in J. Young (ed.) *Celtic dimensions of the British civil wars* (Edinburgh, 1997), p. 3.   **8** The Ulstermen later averred that the Scots 'had taught them their ABC.' The Irish insurgents claimed to be fighting in defence of Charles I and produced a forged warrant purporting to authorise them to seize the kingdom on his behalf.

after the rebellion of 1641 the often antagonistic Gaelic Irish and Old English catholics joined together in the Confederation of Kilkenny.[9] Although a common religion united both groups the confederation was nonetheless deeply, and fatally, divided by political and class difference.[10] Irish Protestants shared a common purpose in their determination to destroy the Irish insurgents but were also riven by faction after the outbreak of civil war in England. Many supported Charles I while others adhered to parliament. James Butler, lord lieutenant of Ireland and later first duke of Ormond, led the royalists but parliament maintained considerable support in Munster having drawn Murrough O'Brien, earl of Inchiquin, away from the king. Parliament also had a strong force acting on their behalf in Ulster after the arrival of Robert Monroe in 1642 with an army of Scottish Covenanters. The Laggan army in Ulster, mainly plantation settlers under the leadership of Sir Robert Stewart, leaned towards royalism but actively co-operated with the Scots against Owen Roe O'Neill and the Gaelic Irish.

The confederates, somewhat cynically it must be said, also pledged allegiance to the king and claimed to be fighting on his behalf.[11] When it became apparent to Charles I that he was losing the war with parliament, he ordered Ormond, whose influence with his supposed confederate enemies was immense, to conclude peace with them in order that he might avail himself of Irish troops. To this end the lord lieutenant had simultaneously been trying to make peace and war with the confederacy from 1643 onwards. The conflict since 1641 had as a result been characterised by shifting allegiances, transitory alliances, truces and cessations of arms, small-scale sieges, summer campaigns, and a few set-piece battles. As a consequence of this desultory but often vicious warfare, by the beginning of 1649 no single group had gained military superiority although it has been estimated that there were between 43,000 and 64,000 men under arms in Ireland by this date.[12]

In England the parliament had defeated the king by 1646 but war broke out again, the Second Civil War, in 1648. An alliance of Scots and the remnants of English royalism was rapidly defeated by parliament's New Model Army under the command of Oliver Cromwell in a lightning campaign in the spring

---

9 For a detailed account of these events see M. Perceval Maxwell, 'Ulster 1641 in the context of political developments in the Three Kingdoms,' in B. Mac Cuarta (ed.), *Ulster 1641: Aspects of the Rising* (Belfast 1993; 2 ed., Belfast 1997), pp 93–106.   10 Recent research has argued that ethnic difference is not a sufficient or even necessary explanation of divisions among the Confederate catholics. Micheál O'Siochru asserts that the primary division was between property and property less, the landless peasantry of Ulster and the landowning gentry and aristocracy in particular. See M. O'Siochru, *Confederate Ireland, 1642–1649: a constitutional and political analysis* (Dublin, 1999), pp 17–18.   11 Their motto was *Pro Deo, rege et patria Hiberni, unanimes.*   12 J., Ohlmeyer (ed.), *Ireland from independence to occupation, 1641–1660* (Cambridge, 1995), p. xxxvi. For a more detailed breakdown see S. Wheeler, 'Four Armies in Ireland,' in Ohlmeyer, pp 43–65, pp 50–1.

and summer of 1648. In December the victorious Independents, crudely the party of the army, purged the Presbyterians from parliament and in January of the following year executed Charles I. They were now free to devote their full attention to the suppression of royalism in Ireland.[13]

By this stage in Ireland, however, the marquis of Ormond had managed to knit together an alliance of anti-parliamentarian forces. In the Second Ormond Peace of January 1649 he managed to come to terms at last with the Irish Confederates who now voluntarily subsumed their government in a pan-Royalist coalition and promised an army of 18,000 men devoted to the king's cause.[14] Some months before his arrival in Ireland, through the good offices of his agent, Colonel John Barry, Ormond also managed to win over the confederates' most formidable and implacable enemy, Murrough O'Brien, earl of Inchiquin, to the cause of Charles I.[15]

The events of January 1649 were to win Ormond his greatest accession of recruits. News of the execution of King Charles I on 30 January galvanised the situation in Ireland. His son, Charles II was immediately declared king but under the rule of the victorious parliament England was for all intents a republic. The Scottish kirk denounced the execution of the king and on 15 February the Ulster presbytery castigated his executioner's as English sectaries, in effect ending the alliance with the English Commonwealth.[16] With the signing of the Ormond Peace the covenanters and royalists now had a common cause, the defeat of the Independents.[17] As the royalist cause advanced and was reinforced by the Ulster covenanters, the authority of the English parliament almost collapsed in Ulster.[18]

II

So, by February 1649 the situation for parliament's forces in Ulster, as in the rest of Ireland, had taken a decided turn for the worse. Although the Ulster presbytery had not so much declared for the new king as declared against the Independent party in the English parliament the result was the same. Their forces were now ranged against those of George Monk and Sir Charles Coote, commanders of the republican forces in Ulster.

---

13 Wheeler, loc. cit., p. 61. 14 The best account of how the Confederacy conducted war can be found in P. Lenihan, 'Celtic' warfare in the 1640s,' in Celtic dimensions of the British civil wars, pp 116-40. 15 Inchiquin signed a truce with the Confederates in May 1648. 16 D. Stevenson, Scottish covenanters and Irish confederates (Belfast, 1981), p. 267. 17 The Presbytery's fundamental disagreement with the Independents who now controlled the English parliament was not particularly the execution of the king but rather the policy of religious toleration pursued by parliament. See R., Bagwell, Ireland under the Stuarts, vol. 2, London, 1909, p. 180. 18 Ibid., p. 268.

Monk's position was precarious but it was not desperate. In England an invasion force of unparalleled strength was being prepared under the leadership of Oliver Cromwell but it could not embark for some months. In the meantime Monk at Dundalk and Drogheda, Coote at Derry and Colonel Michael Jones at Dublin must hold out until the arrival of that army. Above all, they had to retain control of a port or ports at which the army could safely disembark and muster. Aware of the vital importance of the ports, soon after his appointment as governor of Derry, Coote arrested the royalist commander of the city in November 1648.[19] But by the spring of 1649 the parliamentarian garrisons were everywhere under threat. Ormond was moving on Jones at Dublin, the Scots seized the villages and towns in Counties Derry and Donegal and Inchiquin menaced Drogheda and Dundalk. The crisis prompted them to them to think the unthinkable – an alliance with the Gaelic Irish under the command of Owen Roe O'Neill.

Monk was aware that O'Neill's situation would encourage a favourable response from the Irish. The articles of the Ormond Peace between the royalists and confederates proclaimed in mid-January had left Owen Roe isolated from the mainstream royalist forces, holding no rank and with little influence in the new coalition. In August 1648 the supreme council of the confederacy had declared him guilty of treason and an outlaw. In fact, confederate forces had spent much of 1648 trying to destroy O'Neill's forces rather than attacking parliament's troops. The gentry in Ulster had largely withdrawn their support and O'Neill was left to lead an army of landless peasantry. Unpaid, living off the land and poorly armed, his army was disintegrating. Some 2,000 mutinous troops were sent into the service of the Spanish and desertions were rife.[20] Much has been written on what prompted O'Neill to negotiate with

---

19 Stewart's royalist sympathies were well known. Coote and Jones were advised by parliament that he would certainly serve the king and were ordered to secure him. Coote and Monk were well aware of Stewart's politics since all three had served under Ormond and Coote doubtless recalled Ormond's decision to appoint Stewart as governor of Derry instead of the less well inclined Sir William Stewart. Sir Robert was a very capable soldier, a veteran of the Thirty Years War and commanded the strategic fort at Culmore dominating the seaward approaches to the city. It was later thought that Coote had taken the city by storm. In fact he inveigled Stewart to the city to attend a christening and then arrested him and Sir Audley Mervyn: *Dictionary of National Biography*, under Sir Robert Stewart, G. Hill (ed.), *The Montgomery manuscripts*, vol. 1 (Belfast, 1869), note 27, pp 182-3; King to Lords Justices, 9 April 1643, for Sir Robert Stewart, viz. Stewart to be appointed governor of Derry after the death of Sir John Vaughan; *Carte MSS*, v, 62. The author of *A light to the blind* was under the impression that the city had been taken by force by Coote. Describing the poor defences of the city he remarked that 'Scaling the walls is therefore practicable; for it was by that way taken in the wars of Oliver Cromwell' pp 64-5, J.T. Gilbert (ed.), *A Jacobite narrative of the war in Ireland, 1688-91* (2 ed., Shannon, 1971). **20** M. Bennett, *The civil wars in Britain and Ireland, 1638-1651* (Oxford, 1997), p. 309; T.L. Coonan, *The Irish catholic confederation and the puritan revolution* (Dublin, 1954), p. 290.

parliament. The explanations range from fantastic strategic plans to lure the New Model Army to destruction in Ireland and eventually invade England, to the realities of politics in what was obviously the endgame of a long and tortuous war.[21] Clearly, however, explanations for O'Neill's behaviour are more mundane than Machiavellian. Necessity required drastic measures. Owen Roe's priority at this time was to actually keep his army together as a credible military force. As his most recent biographer points out, 'O'Neill and his followers had devoted their lives and fortunes to their cause' and 'only power and might' could have influence in any future settlement.[22] The army was the only means the Ulster Irish had of gaining a voice at the negotiating table, their 'sole safeguard' against utter destruction.[23]

Actually Owen Roe had been negotiating with Ormond since February or March through the agency of his nephew Daniel O'Neill and others but his overtures to Kilkenny were rejected by his enemies in the confederacy. The talks came to nothing partly because of Ormond's inability to deal fairly with the catholic Irish and partly because of the antipathy of the confederate Commissioners of Trust for O'Neill personally and the Ulster Irish in general. The confederate Assembly, now in the guise of the Commissioners of Trust, had seen off the threat of the papal nuncio, Cardinal Rinuccini, whose cause had been supported by O'Neill.[24] They now had no wish to arm his most trusted adherents, the Gaelic Irish forces under Owen Roe. The Irish general had no illusions about what assistance he might receive from that quarter. He told Ormond that 'Their aversion and malice to me and my party are such as that they will study and devise all the ways they can invent to hinder any settlement or union betwixt your Excellency and us.'[25] He tried to negotiate with the royal family, with Queen Henrietta Maria and the young Charles II, sending Francis Nugent to the new king and his mother in exile in France. Together with the earl of Antrim he sounded out Prince Rupert, now in charge of a royalist fleet sent to blockade Jones at Dublin. Pointlessly, Rupert referred him to Ormond.[26] Late in March O'Neill's representatives met those of Ormond to discuss terms but the talks broke up in acrimony with nothing decided. Rebuffed or disappointed at each turn O'Neill looked to his own devices. in April a

21 On O'Neill's supposed strategic plans see T.S. O' Cahan, *Owen Roe O'Neill* (London, 1968), p. 348. The author is of the opinion that O'Neill's motivation for entering into agreements with the parliamentarian commanders was to induce their troops to mutiny and join the royalists, 'his way of winning towns without fighting for them,' since few would be party to a treaty with so detested an enemy as the Gaelic Irish. 22 J.I. Casway, *Owen Roe O'Neill and the struggle for Catholic Ireland* (Philadelphia 1994), pp 242-3. 23 Ibid. 24 Rinuccini left Ireland in February 1649. He had at all times been Ormond's most determined opponent and rejected any attempts at an alliance of confederates and royalists. 25 Coonan, op. cit., p. 291. 26 Casway, op. cit., p. 241.

conference of the Ulster Provincial Council, doubtless at his prompting, gave their general permission to negotiate with Sir Charles Coote at Londonderry.[27]

This decision was not as surprising at it appears at first sight. Since the previous year O'Neill had been negotiating with the council of state at London through Abbot Crelly. In the autumn of 1648 the Gaelic Irish had made a short-term truce of mutual benefit with Jones at Dublin. The Irish supplied the garrison with food and they in turn provided them with powder.[28] When O'Neill was appraised of Coote's situation at Derry, and received a request for assistance from the lord president in April a similar offer was made to him. For O'Neill, such an agreement opened up the possibility of a direct treaty with parliament and was too good to turn down. At this stage, however, Coote refused to countenance an agreement.[29] O'Neill, nonetheless, was aware that the defection of the Scots left Monk vulnerable and determined to take what advantage he could of the situation by proposing a mutual assistance pact. After consultation with Jones Monk admitted that 'his offer is so seasonable that it is now likely I shall be forced to adventure upon it.'[30]

On 8 May O'Neill and Colonel Monk concluded articles of agreement on a cessation of arms for three months between their two armies. They further agreed to assist each other as and where each party thought fit.[31] O'Neill was to receive supply for his forces, the return of the confiscated O'Neill lands, an Act of Oblivion and freedom of worship. These were excellent terms but Monk could afford to be generous. In fact he was well aware that the English parliament could not countenance the implementation of this agreement in full or even in part. During initial negotiations he informed O'Neill, doubtless tongue in cheek, that there were some particulars in his demands which 'might shock and offend the Parliament'.[32] In fact, he realised that none of the articles, except the agreement to supply arms and money, would ever be implemented.[33] Monk was merely trying to gain time until Cromwell could embark with sufficient forces to subdue Ireland.[34] His main object was to prevent

---

27 Ibid., p. 243. 28 The details of Abbot Crelly's shadow negotiations with the Parliament at London are unclear. See Casway, op. cit., p. 243. 29 At this same time Ormond was trying to win Coote and Jones over to the royalist cause. His ham-fisted and insulting overtures, were rejected out of hand by Jones. Coote, however, perhaps held back . J.T. Gilbert, (ed.), *A contemporary history of affairs in Ireland from 1641-1652*, 7 vols., Dublin 1879, vol. I, part 1, p 268. 30 Cited in Casway, p 245. 31 Articles condescended unto, and agreed upon, by and between General Owen O Neal, Commander in Chief of the confederate Catholiques, and Colonel George Monk, Commander in Chief of the Parliament Forces, within the Province of Ulster. Dated 8 May 1649, J.T. Gilbert (ed.), *A contemporary history*, vol. 2, Part 1, pp 216-7. 32 Statements by the Earl of Clarendon, in Gilbert, *Contemporary history*, p. 449. 33 Monk to Cromwell, 25 May 1649; Monk informed Cromwell that O'Neill's propositions were 'wonderful high, but I believe will descend much lower:' Gilbert, pp 221-2. He also requested that Cromwell did not inform the Council of State as yet about this agreement. 34 Monk to Cromwell, 25 May 1649: Gilbert, *Contemporary history*, ibid.

O'Neill or the Ulster Scots royalists joining the marquis of Ormond and capturing the ports, especially Dublin. By making a treaty with O'Neill Monk reasoned,

> that if he could keep the Lord of Ormond and Owen Roe at distance, until supplies arrived, he should not onely deprive the Lord of Ormond of that accession of strength, which Owen Roe's forces would have added unto him, but also render the Scots in Vlster, and the Earl of Clanrickard with his Connaght forces, (all which being joyned together would have made twelve thousand horse and foot) useless to the Lord of Ormond, as to any assistance he could expect from them to joyn against Colonel Jones, Owen Roe lying so with his forces, as that he might within two or three days march, have fallen either into the Scots quarters, or Clanrickards quarters, if the had not kept their forces to attend his motions.[35]

Monk further argued that O'Neill's own situation was so precarious that he would gladly have accepted Ormond's offers 'had he not been speedily prevented.'[36]

In late July Monk requested O'Neill's aid in repulsing Inchiquin who had advanced on Dundalk and promised supply to enable the Irish to take the field. Owen Roe sent General O'Farrell to collect the ammunition promised by Monk from Dundalk. It was at this stage that the deal backfired spectacularly on the English general. Alerted to the presence of the Irish, Inchiquin fell on O'Farrell's force, routed them completely and captured all the supplies. He proceeded immediately to besiege the parliamentarians in Dundalk and forced Monk to surrender the port after his garrison mutinied.[37]

Nonetheless, mutinies apart, the arrangement had served parliament and the Irish well. Dundalk and Drogheda were lost but Ormond's assault on Dublin was much weakened without assistance from O'Neill's infantry. The king's viceroy would soon pay an even heavier price for failing to come to terms with the Irish. For O'Neill, his army was still operational and all had not been

---

35 Gilbert, *Contemporary history* pp 218-219. Above all, Ormond lacked experienced foot, a vital requirement when assaulting a fortified town.   **36** Ibid. Colonel George Monk (1608-1670) was in fact the officer who in 1660 virtually ensured the restoration of Charles II by marching his troops on London. He had begun his career under the marquis of Ormond at the outbreak of the rebellion in 1641 but was captured by parliament at Nantwich in 1644. After a spell in the Tower he accepted a commission from parliament as adjutant-general and governor of Ulster in 1647. For his role in the restoration he was created duke of Albemarle in 1660. For further information see *The Concise Dictionary of National Biography* (Oxford, 1994), vol., 2, p. 2053.   **37** It was reported that the Irish troops were drunk having delayed too long at Dundalk: Casway, op. cit., p. 250.

lost.[38] Monk's lead induced Sir Charles Coote to renew his overtures to O'Neill for a treaty. *Realpolitik* governed the actions of all the commanding generals and all parties were working on the hackneyed cliché that the enemy of my enemy is my friend. For the time being at least, since no one expected an agreement forged by necessity to endure. The fact that it had been concluded in the first place was enough to disgust Edward Hyde, future earl of Clarendon. Hyde, who should have known better, remarked on the moral bankruptcy of both parties: 'these two contrary and disagreeing elements had, I say, by the subtle and volatile spirits of hypocrisy and rebellion, found a way to incorporate together.' If an alliance between O'Neill and Monk appeared appallingly cynical, then that between the former and Sir Charles Coote appears even more surprising.

III

There can be little doubt where Coote's loyalties lay. A second-generation New English settler, he appears to have inherited his father's belief that Catholics, and the Gaelic Irish in particular, were the greatest hindrance to establishing English rule in Ireland. The elder Coote's solution was brutally simple. They should be removed by whatever means possible. His preferred method, implemented to the full after the outbreak of the Rebellion in 1641, was to massacre the Irish, the guilty and innocent alike, at every opportunity. Indeed, it could be argued that Coote's depredations on the Old English community were instrumental in fomenting rebellion by spreading fear and disaffection. So notorious and barbaric were his activities that it was rumoured after his death in 1642 that he had been assassinated on the orders of his commanding officer, the earl of Ormond, rather than killed by the Irish.[39] Like his father, Coote the younger had decidedly parliamentarian sympathies but he served with distinction, and familiar inhumanity, under the royalist Ormond against the Confederates.[40] In 1645 he was appointed lord president of Connacht and threw in his lot with the Cromwellians.

38 Cf. Richard Bagwell: 'Each of these two silent men, [Monk and O'Neill] who were soldiers and not politicians, thought the preservation of his army the first object,' *Ireland under the Stuarts* (London, 1909), vol. 2, p. 182. 39 W.P. Kelly, 'The early career of James Butler, 12th earl and 1st duke of Ormond, 1610-1643' (unpublished PhD thesis, Cambridge University), 1995, p. 213. Sir Charles had decided sympathies with the parliament in England and acted on a number of occasions against the interests of the royalist party led by Ormond. His epitaph perhaps best illustrates his own and others' perception of his career: 'England's honour, Scotland's wonder, Ireland's terror here lies under.' Lady W. Burghclere, *The life of James, first duke of Ormonde, 1610-1688*, (London, 1912), vol. 1, p. 181. 40 After capturing Sligo in 1645 he massacred the entire garrison, M., Bennett, op. cit., p. 330; Coote was described by Irish sources as 'that inhuman bloodsucker,' *Contemporary history*, vol. 3, p. 88; C.P. Meehan, *The confederation of*

In December 1648 Coote seized Derry on behalf of the parliament and arrested the leading royalists, Sir Robert Stewart and Sir Audley Mervyn. When the Ulster presbytery broke off relations with parliament, Coote declined an offer to join them.[41] Anticipating an attack he began to strengthen the fortifications at Derry early in 1649. Forces from the Laggan army loosely invested the city from February onwards but actual hostilities broke out at the end of March when Sir Alexander Stewart's troops of the Laggan army seized the villages of Carrigans and Manorcunningham on the outskirts of the city cutting the Derry garrison off from their supply routes.[42] From this date on the city was effectively blockaded for the next five months.

We know about the events of the siege because one of Coote's officers, Captain Henry Finch, an alderman of the city, left a diary in two letters to a correspondent in London dated 19 June and 15 August 1649.[43] In his diary Finch describes in some detail the military operations carried out by both sides. He was much less forthcoming on the political motivations and aims of the opposing forces but what is interesting is the terminology he used to describe the different parties. He ascribed the onset of hostilities in late March and early April to 'a generall revolt of all the Scotch [*sic*]' but left it to his audience to conclude, as they certainly would, that they had 'revolted' against the English parliament. As conflict intensified over the coming months, Finch, as we shall see, appears to have refined his analysis of exactly who was fighting who at Derry until eventually the 'English, Scotch and Irish', royalists are subsumed under the heading of the 'British'.

Throughout April skirmishing continued around the city, 'upon the strand beyond the gallows', and 'by the bogge side', with a number of casualties on both sides although the besieging forces usually came off worst in these encounters.[44] On 23 April the republicans sallied out and heavily defeated the Laggan forces at Carrigans in Donegal, killing sixteen including two senior officers, taking forty prisoners and capturing eight colours, with no loss to their own force. This and other victories by Coote's forces were later reported in England, incongruously to modern eyes, as *A bloody fight in Ireland, and a great victory obtained by Sir Charles Coote, Lord President of Connaught, and commander of those forces, and of Londonderry, against the British forces of Laggan, with some Regiments of Irish and Highlanders under Major-General Monro.*[45]

Kilkenny (Dublin, 1882), p. 272.   **41** J.S. Reid, *History of the Presbyterian church in Ireland*, W.D. Killen, ed., 3 vols., Belfast 1867, p. 103.   **42** Reid, op. cit., p. 104.   **43** The letters are reprinted in Gilbert, *Contemporary history*, pp 440-6. The letters were printed as broadsheets and used by parliament in their propaganda war against their opponents.   **44** Ibid., pp 440-1. Finch himself was captured on one occasion but soon exchanged for an enemy prisoner.   **45** 23 April, Finch, 'A party of 50 horse of ours being no more officers and all, marched to Cargans, where the generall randezvouze of the Scotch then was, 40 of our musketeers went out to make good their horse retreate but went not a mile off, where we tooke 45 prisoners, killed 16, whereof one Maj.

These operations notwithstanding, Coote's position was still insecure and isolated. By early May the royalist forces were entrenched in strength within cannon range of the city and the republicans were forced to prepare for an intensified investment The garrison demolished the cabins and houses outside the city walls and cut down the orchards to deny cover to the enemy forces.[46] No determined attacks were made to assault the city in May but skirmishing and raiding continued while the royalists awaited reinforcement. Indeed, Finch was of the opinion that the siege would have been lifted had not Sir Robert Stewart and Sir Audley Mervyn arrived with more men on 26 May.[47] After this date siege operations began in earnest. Within the week the royalists 'had built an incredible peece of work within almost musket shot of our towne, upon the top of the hill upon the way of Ballymackerooty [Ballymagroarty].' Coote overran the fort the following day but the royalist managed to demolish defensive outworks at the Windmill only some hundreds of yards from the walls.[48]

Nonetheless the besiegers faced a difficult task not least because Coote had had the foresight as far back as February to ensure the town was fully equipped for a siege. The garrison was well supplied with food, weapons and ammunition.[49] The besieging forces, a unlikely combination of Presbyterian covenanters, Catholic and Protestant royalists, confederates, 'English, Scotch and Irish', as Finch put it, were riven by traditional and factional disputes. They were jointly commanded by Sir Alexander Stewart and Lord Montgomery of Ards, a notoriously blasphemous and often foul-mouthed opponent of the covenant who had a fondness for drink. He was, in fact, the very antithesis of Presbyterian sobriety and had only been given command on the grounds of a supposed reformation in religion, politics and habit.[50]

Belfore an able souldier, and a wise man, and another Captaine, 30 and odd of the prisoners were exchanged for so many boules of meale, the rest being Lieu. Col. James Galbraith; 2 majors, 1 Captain and other Officers and Country men, who are reserved for ransome or other ends; brought eight colours, and narrowly escaped many other Commanders, and all this without loss of one man, one hurt': B. Lacy, *Siege city. A history of Derry and Londonderry* (2 ed., Belfast 1995), p. 107. 46 Finch, ibid. 47 Finch, ibid. Stewart had managed to escape from custody at London in January: *DNB*, vol. 54, p. 345. 48 Finch, p. 442. 49 A measure of how comfortably off the garrison was is evidenced by Finch's remark that on 3 June 'The cows being too many to keep for eating up our grasse, and not fit to kill, so many as were not usefull, was sold to the enemy for 10s a peece, upon parrole and was currantly paid': pp 441–2. On 19 June the garrison also captured shipping bound for Scotland. Moreover, the garrison had already laid up supplies in expectation of a siege: 'It is not without great providence of God, that salt beef, herring, salt cod, salt salmon, at the time of the year drinking little (some nothing) but water, should prove so nourishing as it doth, and not rather breed diseases': pp 442–3; Apart from what they managed to capture the garrison received supplies of wheat from London. 50 Adair, cited at Reid, asserts that after the death of Charles I, 'Lords Claneboy and Ards, with their officers, did generally, and with great alacrity renew the covenant. Yea, the made a show of some reformation for a time, restraining all drinking, swearing, and profane courses, as had been usual among them. They entertained the ministers kindly, and did much simulate strictness; but still

It would appear that Lord Montgomery in particular found it difficult to maintain the pretence and rapidly reverted to his old politics and ungodly ways. On arrival with his troops before Derry, after an apparently very convivial dinner with Coote at Derry, he returned to his camp much the worse for drink and declared that if Coote would declare for the king, 'the devil take him that meddles with religion; let God fight for his own religion Himself!'[51] Coote was reinforced at the end of June, when his brother, Richard, arrived from Connaught. However, while these men may have been of assistance at Derry, after they had left Sligo the garrison there deserted to the royalist cause. Nonetheless they had arrived at Derry in the nick of time.

On 7 July Colonel George Munroe, who had been engaged in mopping up operations in County Derry and elsewhere, was able to add his considerable force of 300-400 cavalry, 1500 foot and 12 artillery pieces to those already entrenched before the city. This new accession of strength, especially the cannon, allowed the besiegers to build a fort, Charlesfort, near Culmore, near where the boom was constructed during the siege of 1689, to cut the city off from re-supply by sea. The royalists' plan appears to have been to starve the city into submission and on 20 July they withdrew their troops from the entrenchments closest to the walls. They hoped also to draw the often impetuous Coote into a decisive engagement against the superior numbers outside the walls and drew up on a number of occasions before the city.[52] On 26 July Lord Ards returned to city with a commission from Charles II and reinforcements which he drew up before the walls and summoned the garrison to surrender.[53] A full-scale assault on the walls on 28 July was repulsed with considerable loss to the royalists. Disheartened by this setback and uncomfortable with an alliance with Catholics, Presbyterian forces began to disengage in the days after.[54] After Montgomery's admission of his warrant from Charles II and Ormond his army dwindled away before his eyes.

After the departure of the covenanting troops Coote became more active, his forces burned 'Carganes, Sir John Cunningham's Newtown, Colmactreene and St Johnstown', in early August. Clearly, nearly four months into the siege, Coote's small garrison was still capable of resolute action against the royalists. The desertion of the Covenanters from the besieging army had improved his tactical situation but strategically, he was still isolated. Montgomery and Ards

with a secret intention to espouse the old quarrel in the person of the young king': cited in Reid, pp 91-2. Alexander Stewart was a nephew of Sir Robert Stewart. 51 Adair, cited at Reid, p. 107. 52 Coote had only 800 foot and 150 horse available to him, *The Montgomery manuscripts*, vol. 1, note 48, p. 189. 53 Finch, p. 444. 54 The Presbyterians were outraged when Ards claimed his authority for the king. Many of them were especially concerned at the Catholic Highland and Irish troops under Munroe's command. They alleged that Munroe's capture of Coleraine and Carrickfergus was accomplished on behalf of the marquis of Ormond and against the covenant. Adair, cited at Reid, p. 110.

had taken Belfast, Coleraine and Carrickfergus. Inchiquin had taken Dundalk and Jones' situation at Dublin, surrounded by royalists troops under the marquis of Ormond looked dangerously insecure. Moreover, it was entirely possible that further reinforcements and a sustained assault could overwhelm the small garrison at Derry. Even before the covenanters had withdrawn from Derry, following the example of Jones and Monck, Coote renewed his overtures to O'Neill and reopened the negotiations suspended since April.[55] His own reservations notwithstanding, he was ordered by parliament to do whatever was necessary to bring the campaign to a successful conclusion.

Coote's despatches reached O'Neill at Clones on 24 July where he had sought refuge after O'Farrell's defeat by Inchiquin.[56] O'Neill immediately agreed to help. He did so for three reasons. In the first place he needed supply for his army and Coote promised thirty barrels of powder and three hundred head of cattle.[57] Secondly, and perhaps more important by this stage, the capture of Derry by royalist troops would have isolated O'Neill's army completely and 'prove of verie dangerous consequence for him, and in a maner impossible to subsiste.'[58] Since May, Ormond's generals, Castlehaven and Preston, had captured his garrisons at Maryborough and Athy.[59] Finally, the cessation agreed with Coote for three months effectively renewed his agreement with parliament since his previous engagement with Monk was at term. O'Neill was also negotiating with Ormond and the parliamentarians suspected that if he were not joined with them he would certainly join with Ormond once his agreement with Monk lapsed on 26 July. A hapless parliamentarian officer reported just as much to Jones in early July. He related also that O'Neill's men were still under attack from the Ormondists and admitted that he was perplexed: 'Jugling there is among them, which I cannot unriddle.'[60]

On reaching agreement O'Neill, 'marched by short steps with his army, consisting of 2,000 men, 'till he came to Ballykelly in the county of Derry, of which he possessed himself. The Scots, hearing of his approach, raised their siege and posted away by day and night, 'till the were over the Ban-water in their own country.'[61] On 8 August, at Coote's invitation, this *bête noir* of the English attended a banquet at Derry in his honour. While the evening can hardly have been the most convivial of affairs, widely reported allegations that

55 O'Neill's Journal, Gilbert, *Contemporary history*, p. 211.   **56** Casway, p. 250; O'Neill's Journal, *Contemporary history*, p. 213.   **57** Casway, ibid.   **58** Gilbert, *Contemporary history*, p. 41.   **59** Some measure of the fate which awaited O'Neill's men at the hands of their erstwhile allies is revealed by Monk's report of the fall of Maryborough to Cromwell informing him that Ormond, 'hath taken a garrison of Own Mac Arts, and put most of the men to the sword,' George Monk to Oliver Cromwell, Dundalk, 25 May 1649, Gilbert, *Contemporary history*, pp 221-2.   **60** Letter to Colonel Michael Jones on movements in Ireland, 3 July 1649, Gilbert, *Contemporary history*, pp 222-3.   **61** O'Neill's Journal, *Contemporary history*, p. 211.

Coote took the opportunity to poison his guest are probably untrue.[62] Certainly, however, both men knew that this temporary alliance would rapidly collapse once the situation had altered in favour of either. O'Neill was met at Ballykelly by his nephew, Daniel O'Neill, acting as agent for Ormond, who proposed a new alliance with the king's lord lieutenant.[63] The negotiations were largely irrelevant: the day after the Irish relieved Derry Jones routed the royalist forces at Rathmines in a victory from which they never recovered.[64] The way was clear for Cromwell to land his army.

                                            I V

Obviously, this siege had important consequences in Ireland. Why then is it by and large forgotten in the history and folk memory of Ulster? Perhaps it is because it was historically unimportant with no particular consequences, an isolated event with no effect on the overall struggle in these islands? It is argued that 1689 not only facilitated the landing of troops under Marshal Schomberg but in fact prevented an invasion of Scotland and England by the Jacobites, and therefore ensured the survival of the 'Glorious Revolution.' English parliamentary democracy, it is sometimes argued, owes its very existence to the defenders of Derry in 1689. Judging by the scant historiography it would appear that the outcome of 1649 had little or no impact on future events. But, for that matter neither did the siege of 1689. Had the Jacobites captured the city, it is suggested, they would have went on to invade Scotland. But it is almost certain that in the unlikely event of them ever arriving in Scotland they would have been swiftly crushed. Moreover, the siege of 1649 did result in a number of important consequences for the war in Ireland. Crucially, it diverted O'Neill and the Ulster army at a time when his intervention at Dublin may have proved decisive. It therefore assisted the parliamentarians in maintaining control of the ports. Had Derry been taken Ormond envisaged using the royalist troops of the Laggan army to attack Dublin and, in his biographer's opinion, captured the city. The alliance of O'Neill and Coote 'proved very fatal to the king's affairs, and hindered the lord lieutenant from being reinforced by a body of troops which might have enabled him to reduce Dublin before the

---

62 According to Irish sources he took the opportunity to present his guest with 'a cupp of poyson. . .of lingringe operation,' which resulted in O'Neill's death shortly after, 'his haire and nailes fallinge off by degrees. AD p. 42; It was reported that O'Neill feared that he was to be assassinated by the celebrated poisoner, Bottle Smith, who had arrived in Derry on a ship from Dublin in June, O'Cahan, *Owen Roe O'Neill*, p. 354. 63 Daniel O'Neill to Ormond, Balle Kelly, 5 September, 1649. A consummate diplomat, Daniel O'Neill's nickname was 'Infallible Subtle.' For further information seeD.F., Cregan, 'An Irish cavalier: Daniel O'Neill,' *Studia Hibernica*, 3, (1963), pp 60-100; i4, (1964), pp 104-33; 5, (1965), pp 42-77. 64 Coonan, op. cit., p 293.

arrival of Cromwell, or made it difficult for that regicide to land his forces in the neighbourhood.'[65] Ormond actually requested Prince Rupert, in command of the royalist navy, to block up the port of Derry. The lord lieutenant argued that parliament's frigates destined to transport troops to Jones would be diverted to Derry and 'The interruption which might be given to that access of strength to Jones would in all probability render that work against him very easy, whereas, on the contrary, if he was supplied, it would be almost a desperate undertaking, and himself should be forced to a defensive war.'[66]

So, from parliament's view, if all else failed and Dublin fell, Derry at least still held out for Cromwell's invasion force. O'Neill's forces, interminable disputes among the Irish Confederates notwithstanding, might very well have allied with the marquis of Ormond and defeated the Cromwellians under Jones at Dublin. Defeat at Dublin at this stage, when the royalists held almost all of Ireland, would have had incalculable results, given the fraught political situation in England. But orthodoxy agrees in this at least: both sieges tied down armies that might have been better occupied elsewhere. Ironically, the events of 1649 may have contributed to Williamite victory in 1689-90. Dr Gorges, governor of Derry in the 1660's, pointed out at the beginning of that war that just as in 1649 Enniskillen and Londonderry were the only English garrisons in Ulster. He recommended that the tactics and strategies used so successfully by Coote in 1649 to defeat his enemies, were just as viable in 1689, especially retaining a base at Londonderry.[67]

Nor can it be that the siege was a less significant event in terms of military operations. It is true that both 'sieges' have all the appearance of blockades but both were full-scale military operations. The 1649 siege was longer in duration if not intensity than that of 1689 and lasted some seventeen weeks from the end of March until O'Neill approached on 7 August. The later siege lasted 105 days, and, if the time of close blockade is taken into account, an even shorter time. The armies of 1649 were as well if not better armed and equipped than those of 1689, especially the besieging forces. The battles at Derry in 1649 were, however, fought by seasoned professional soldiers rather than the citizen militia and ragbag of Irish Jacobite troops who faced each other in 1689. All parties to the conflict in 1649 had been engaged in combat since 1641 and all had a number of significant military honours already under their belts.

Tactics were nonetheless virtually the same. Military operations followed roughly the same pattern – skirmishing and assaults on the walls. Direct attacks were vigorously resisted. With one crucial difference – experienced

65 T., Carte, *The life of James, duke of Ormonde* (2 ed., 6 vols., Oxford 1851), vol. 3, p. 463. **66** Ormond to Sir Robert Stewart, 29 April 1649, cited at Carte, op. cit., p. 442. **67** Considerations concerning the Government of Ireland,' 13-14 June, 1689, *HMC, Finch MSS* (London, 1922), vol. 2, pp 216-17. Colonel Gorges was governor of Londonderry from September 1661: *DNB*, Stewart entry.

republican troops, unlike the defenders of 1689, sallied out some distance from the city to attack enemy supply lines and re-supply themselves. The besieging forces surrounded the city and attempted to blockade Lough Foyle.

What is also certain is that the earlier siege was fought as bitterly as the later. Casualties among the defenders were lower than they were in 1689, Finch's Diary reveals less than twenty killed in battle and some thirty of forty of O'Neill's men. According to the same source the toll among the besiegers was some 120 killed. During the siege of 1689 only some eighty or ninety soldiers and civilians were killed defending the city or by artillery. Jacobite casualties are not known but they would have been considerably higher. The high casualty toll in 1689 was mostly caused by starvation, privation and disease. In 1649 very few combatants or civilians on both sides died of any of these – both forces were well supplied with provisions. So, if both sieges had profound consequences and both were of comparable and intensity we must look elsewhere for the reasons why 1649 is largely forgotten.

The siege of 1649 was an historically important event. So why is it never commemorated and historiographically almost invisible? The argument here is that there are essentially three main reasons. Firstly, 1649 does not have the mythic potential of 1689. Secondly, this siege is ideologically problematic in explaining the history of Ulster loyalism and, indeed, Irish nationalism. Finally, it occurred during a period of British history which even, or especially, some English historians who generated the myth of 1689, preferred to forget. The interplay of these three factors produced the tendency to neglect or ignore the complex events of 1649.

Part of the explanation lies in the casualty figures outlined above. It is the number of civilian dead in the later siege which gives a clue to the relative unimportance, as myth, of the siege of 1649. While we can agree that as a military operation the siege of 1689 was itself insignificant in military terms compared to that of Limerick in the following two years or the great sieges on the continent, the enormous suffering of ordinary people during the siege of Derry, the numbers who died of starvation and disease, was a sacrifice of heroic proportions.

History needs myths. Myths make history understandable, they make it memorable and a part of daily life. 1689 is the foundation myth of Ulster unionism. In A.T.Q. Stewart's words, 'the epic of the Protestant plantation [providing] its enduring watchword, "No Surrender."' McDonagh described these events as the 'original and most powerful myth of Ulster loyalism'.[68] Myths and legends nonetheless need to be grounded in fact, however tenuous

---

68 *DNB*, vol.54, op. cit., p. 61; O. McDonagh, *States of mind: a study of Anglo-Irish conflict,* 1780-1980 (London, 1983), p. 14 cited in I. McBride, *The siege of Derry in Ulster Protestant mythology* (Dublin, 1997), p. 10.

the relation. The most important and enduring pre-1689 myth of Ulster protestantism is the allegations of widespread massacre accompanying the outbreak of the rebellion in October 1641. The recurring nightmare for protestants from this era is not 1649 but the undoubted horrors of 1641 elevated to the status of myth by reiteration in every generation since, especially at times of crisis.[69] The disappearance of 1649 is in stark contrast to the continued power of the 1641 myth. Why this is so is clear. Sixteen forty-one, like 1689 but unlike 1649 encapsulates the fundamental themes of the loyalist myth. As Ian McBride has pointed out, the themes of 'defiance, solidarity, sacrifice and deliverance' are present in both cases.[70]

There were military casualties in 1649 but the terrible privations and suffering endured by the people of Derry, almost all civilian, were mercifully absent in 1649. Nor was there any sustained bombardment of the city. In other words the ingredients of a heroic sacrifice were not present in 1649.[71] As we shall see, there are even more problems with some other components of the myth.The fact that casualties in 1649 were not on a scale to merit elevation to the status of myth is alone not responsible for this exercise in selective memory. Solidarity, the myth of a monolithic protestantism, standing resolutely regardless of sectarian or theological difference, against the threat of catholic domination, was clearly not the case in 1649. Protestant killed protestant at Carrigans as enthusiastically as they had killed the Irish before and after. In 1689, the myth asserts, Presbyterians and Church of Ireland sank their differences in the face of a common foe. The siege of 1689, and the events of the Williamite war, read in outline, superficially and parochially rather than geopolitically, are at least more amenable to reductionist sectarian argument. Did not a Protestant king supported by Protestant nations and English, Irish and Scots Protestants defeat a Catholic king supported by the Catholic Scots and Irish, and, of course, the French?

Of course, this is not what happened. During the siege of Derry, sectarian enmity and rancour amongst Protestants were the cause of mutinies, accusations and counter-accusations of cowardice and betrayal.[72] Undoubtedly the burden of resistance was borne by the Presbyterians, the better sort having the

69 B. MacCuarta (ed.), *Ulster 1641. Aspects of the rising* (Belfast, Institute of Irish Studies, rev. ed., 1997), p. 6-7 and passim. Sir John Temple's, *The Irish rebellion* (London, 1643) is still mined as a source by loyalist commentators. For a particularly striking example of this genre see B.A., Campbell, *Remember 1641* (Belfast, 1995). This latest edition is one of four published in the present decade. **70** McBride, p. 12. **71** Although some historians have questioned whether the blockade of the city in 1689 actually amounted to a siege and stress the inability of the Jacobites to maintain a sustained assault there is no question that the inhabitants of the city died in their thousands. See, H., Belloc, *James II* (London, 1928), Sir Charles, Petrie, 'The Jacobite War in Ireland, 1688-91,' in *New English Review* vol. 15/1, (July 1947) and most recently, Richard, Doherty, *The Williamite war in Ireland, 1688-91* (Dublin, 1998). **72** McBride, p. 27.

means and inclination to flee the advancing Jacobites. Many of the 'better sort,' including the Bishop Hopkins, had fled to Scotland before this, leaving the ordinary people to shift for themselves.[73] They had the means to leave. Their tenantry did not. These differences rapidly surfaced into acrimonious public argument immediately after the relief of the city.[74] But 1649 raises even more problems than religious rivalry amongst Protestants. Above all, it reveals how national self-interest, not religion, was the paramount factor influencing events.

The brief alliance of O'Neill and Coote against the Laggan forces proved that English interests were and are not necessarily British interests. Moreover, as Richard Bagwell pointed out, 'the English interest could evidently only be preserved by the English'.[75] What happened at one level at Derry in 1649 was that the 'English', as opposed to the 'British', were quite prepared to come to a tactical arrangement with those they had recently declared to be enemies unto death, to gain a strategic advantage. These were the very same people who, the myth of 1641 alleges, were those followers of the Antichrist who had inflicted unheard of cruelties on the settler population of Ulster.[76] None of the parties to the deals struck between O'Neill, Coote and Monk were under any illusions about the objectives of the other. Coote was prepared to countenance not merely negotiation with the Irish, whom the Laggan forces had now been fighting for some eight years, but an alliance with Owen Roe O'Neill.[77]

It is also significant in this regard that Finch ascribed the onset of hostilities to 'a generall revolt of all the Scotch'. The idea that the Scots were the prime movers in the revolt against parliament also has implications for the solidarity of the Ulstermen. The crowns of England and Scotland had been united in 1603 but to the English administration at Dublin in the seventeenth

---

73 One commentator reported that the mayor David Cairnes was forced to write 'to several persons of note, who had fled in panic to Castledoe, for the purpose of embarking there for Scotland,' imploring them not to desert the city. His efforts were fruitless. J. Graham, *Derriana* (Londonderry, 1843), p. 40.   74 See, for example, Governor Walker's blatantly self-promotional account of these events, *A true account of the siege of London-Derry* (London and Edinburgh, 1689) and the Presbyterian riposte, J. MacKenzie, *A narrative of the siege of Londonderry: or the late memorable transactions of the City. Faithfully represented to rectifie the mistakes, and supply the omissions of Mr Walker's account* (London, 1690). The debate continued after Walker was raised to the see of Derry: Walker, *A vindication of the true account of the siege of Derry in Ireland* (London, 1689), MacKenzie, *Dr Walker's invisible champion foyl'd: wherein all the arguments offered in a late pamphlet to prove it a false libel, are examin'd and refuted,* (London, 1690). Walker was killed at the battle of the Boyne in this same year.   75 R. Bagwell, *Ireland under the Stuarts,* vol. 2, (London, 1909), p. 180.   76 For an account of the background to Protestant views of the Irish see A. Clarke, 'The 1641 rebellion and anti-popery in Ireland,' in MacCuarta, pp 139-57.   77 In the immediate aftermath of the relief of the city protestant garrisons which had held out throughout the rebellion fell to the Irish forces. See Finch, Diary, in *Contemporary history,* pp 440-6.

century, the Scots, Protestant and Catholic, were often viewed as rivals and competitors, even enemies, rather than allies.

What happened in 1649 was that political ideology, pragmatism or *Realpolitik* took precedence over religion. A sensible concern to preserve life and property was certainly active among all parties in both sieges. Coote allied with O'Neill to save city and garrison while the unjustly notorious Colonel Robert Lundy would have come to terms with the Jacobites in 1689 had he been given the opportunity. Preservation rather than heroic death was the aim in mind. The lessons from 1649 were that Irish protestants were as divided as Irish catholics. Worse, some of them were in league with papists.

One other theme to the myth is that of deliverance or salvation from the hands of enemies, in 1689 through the temporal intervention of Kirke's fleet but with undeniable assistance from the hand of God, on behalf of his chosen people. But in 1649, who delivered who? Owen Roe certainly delivered Coote and may very well have contributed to the deliverance of Dublin from Ormond. Inexplicably, in terms of the doctrine of a chosen people, God was apparently on every side but that of the godly. The eventual victors, Coote and the parliamentarians were actually assisted by followers of the Antichrist in the person of O'Neill and the Ulster Irish. After the arrival of Cromwell, Coote and Venables later swept all before them in Ulster.

We might add to McBride's four key elements of the siege myth one other, that of betrayal. The traitor Lundy is an integral aspect of the myth of 1689. The people of Londonderry *saved themselves* when all others had deserted them. They can therefore only rely on their own people and their own resources. Sixteen forty-nine, however, requires one to answer difficult questions about just whom one can rely on. Certainly not those protestants who joined with the Englishman Coote and his garrison. The insecurity, the fear of betrayal, which lies at the root of the so-called 'siege mentality' is grounded on the premise that betrayal has happened in the past and could happen again at any time. Constant vigilance is required to ensure that Protestant, British Ulster will not once more be left to look to its own devices when the English have come to an arrangement with the Irish. The problem at Derry in 1649 was that there were numerous Lundy's and since Sir Charles Coote and the Cromwellians eventually won the day no fitting scapegoat can be found.

Myth only works if it is relevant to ideology and history is only of use if it serves the myth. This is perhaps why, in Maria Laffan's phrase, it is often easier to invent than to remember accurately. Perhaps the main reason why 1649 is largely forgotten is that it cannot serve the needs of a myth which underpins an ideology of struggle, separateness, solidarity, sacrifice, betrayal etc. So-called 'siege mentality' demands the suspension of pragmatism and the retreat into myth. As A.T.Q. Stewart asserts, there have been Lundy's in every generation since 1689. In this regard it is also significant that nationalists do not celebrate or remember these events. They too are embroiled in the myth of 1689 and are often loathe to contemplate the implications of what happened at Derry in 1649. For one thing O'Neill's alliance with Coote upsets the comfortable notion of posterity that the indomitable Ulster Gaels would never brook any compromise with the English. Least of all Oliver Cromwell, that monster of nationalist myth, who slaughtered the people of Drogheda and Wexford, and drove the Irish 'to Hell or Connaught'. It is of course disconcerting to contemplate a great O'Neill in alliance with Coote, the son of a man whose name had become synonymous in Ireland with brutality and butchery of the most appalling nature. Perhaps this is the reason why allegations that Sir Charles assassinated O'Neill appear to have so much credence even now. The poisoning story sweetens the pill, so to speak, for nationalist historians. English perfidy is confirmed and the guilty party, while still a great Irishman, paid the penalty for compromising with the traditional enemy. Sir Charles later remarked on his alliance with O'Neill that to do the Lord's work 'it is sometimes necessary to make use of evil instruments.'[78] Owen Roe also had explanations to make. To Pope Innocent X he argued that he viewed an alliance with the Ormondists or the parliamentarians with 'God knows with the same hatred and horror, but under priessure of necessity, or one thing or the other will have to be done by us necessarily and soon unless reasonable aid rescues us from that position.'[79] For both Coote and O'Neill necessity made strange bedfellows.

The problem with 1649 for contemporary readings of Irish history was and is that it generates more questions than answers, questions too complex to be answered by linear ideological explanation based on sectarian division. In all its complexity it cannot therefore feed the needs of the myth. In this sense 1649 is redundant history and this is why it will not be commemorated by unionists

---

78 O'Neill and his army were described in England as, 'bloody Roe,' an 'incarnate devil,' and 'blood quaffing cannibals,' Casway, p. 247; Coote was under no obligation to explain his actions other than to his troops. He had permission from parliament to engage in a treaty with O'Neill. A House of Commons Commission specifically stated that they are satisified that his actions taken 'for the interest of the Commonwealth of England.' Gilbert, *Contemporary history* appendix p. 447, Commons vote 24 August 1649. 79 Casway, p. 246. 80 It has been argued here that one of the major problems with the siege of 1649 is that, unlike 1689, it is not amenable to reductionist argument. The complexity of the situation in Ireland, in Britain in fact, would frustrate the efforts of even the most determined reductionist to present these events as a battle between Catholics and Protestants. Undaunted, however, some heroic souls have tried, with farcical, if well intended results. Recently it was suggested in the *Derry Journal* in an attempt to end the annual battle over parades that the events of the 1649 siege could instead be commemorated as a point of cultural confluence between Protestants and Catholics in Northern Ireland. Did not a Catholic army rescue a Protestant army? To celebrate these events, it was proposed that The Apprentice Boys and the Ancient Order of Hibernians could walk the walls together.

or nationalists in Ulster.[80] The ideological problems of Ulster loyalism in particular but for Irish nationalism also, are that polarities in Ulster were and are not binary and any attempt to explain 1649 in these terms reveals the poverty of the myth. For loyalism also, there are further problems. The unfortunate tendency of Presbyterianism to partner with the strangest of bedfellows and the even more distressing propensity of the English, the senior partners in a supposedly Protestant alliance, to follow their own best interests regardless of the loyal population of Ireland, has been a recurrent problem for unionism.

In fact the myth of 1689 was in great part created by an English historian as part of the justification for the so-called Glorious Revolution, an English civil war which finished the business with the monarchy begun in the 1640s. 'Whig' history was also loathe to contemplate these events. If 1688 was a 'Glorious Revolution,' the Puritan Revolution of the 1640's was best forgotten as an abberation. Lord Macaulay is the man credited more than most with creating the myth of the siege of Londonderry. He certainly did more than most to construct the idea of protestant solidarity in the face of Catholic absolutism. There was of course no such solidarity, either inside the walls, in Ulster, in Ireland or in Britain.[81] But this interpretation is of course more amenable to a reductionist reading of events. It would bedevil the efforts of even the most determined reductionist to explain what happened at Derry in 1649 as merely a religious conflict. In the nineteenth century, the heroic tale of the defence of Londonderry against supposedly overwhelming odds served its ideological purpose in demonstrating the ineluctable progress of the English nation to its destiny. What happened at Derry in 1689 was that tyranny was defeated and liberty triumphed. It is remarkable that these commemorations today, and the accompanying marches with their attendant security apparatus, dispute and argument are a source of baffled wonderment to most people in Britain.

In the end the great losers of 1649 were ironically those who had contributed to Coote's victory at Derry. The tragedy for the Ulster Irish was that in the end they gained little or nothing from their alliance. While aid for them never materialised, Cromwell landed at Dublin on 15 August with an army which eventually overcame resistance. Reinforced in Ulster Coote and Colonel Venables swept all before them. Within months of relieving Derry the army that O'Neill had maintained against all odds for some seven years met the parliamentarians at Scarrifhollis outside Letterkenny on 1 June 1650. Incompetently led by Bishop Eibher MacMahon the Irish gave battle against the advice of Owen Roe's son, Henry, and were slaughtered in the rout that followed.[82] After the battle, Coote repaid in full O'Neill's assistance of the previous year. One of those captured after surrendering on terms was Henry

---

81 On this cf J.R. Young, below, pp 53–74.   82 O'Neill's Journal, Gilbert, *Contemporary history*, p. 213.

O'Neill. O'Neill asked that Coote take what revenge he sought on him alone and reminded him of his alliance with his father some months before. Coote, however, answered that 'if your father and you haue don me a courtesie I payed you for it, and therefore doe not trouble yourselfe, my judgement shall pass, and there is an end, which was done as formerlie'. Coote ordered that his prisoner be beaten to death with tent poles but 'being observed by one of Sir Charles's officers that was coming towards the tent, asked the soldiers what they meant by using a gentleman so, and they replying, it was by the general's orders, the officer, in compassion to him, and to put him out of pain, drew his sword and ran him through the heart.'[83] O'Neill's head was cut off and fixed on the gibbet at Derry alongside that of Bishop MacMahon, who had been hanged, drawn and quartered.

Sir Charles later went on to welcome Charles II back as king at the Restoration in 1660. Aidan Clarke's explanation of his motives for doing so in 1660 might just as well stand as an explanation of the actions of all the parties at Derry in 1649: 'Coote's behaviour, often occluded, contradictory and fumbling . . . hints at the erratic interplay of opportunism, principle, ambition and older feuds' which characterised the politics of the seventeenth century as much as religious difference.[84]

---

83 O'Neill's Journal, Gilbert, *Contemporary History*; There are differing accounts as to exactly where and how Henry O'Neill was killed but all agree that he was put to death either at Derry or on the field at Scarrifhollis.   84 A. Clarke, '1659 and the road to restoration,' in Ohlmeyer, *Ireland from Independence*, p. 231.

The Scottish response to the siege of Londonderry, 1689-90

John R. Young

The siege of Londonderry has remained an important historical icon in the complex relationship between Scotland and Ulster in terms of the development of modern Scottish society. Its symbolism has remained unabated in parts of the Scottish Protestant psyche.[1] Scotland and Ulster have been bound together by successive waves of migration across the North Channel in both directions to create a strong cultural and ethnic link over the centuries. By the late seventeenth century Scottish Presbyterians were the dominant ethnic group in Ulster based on successive waves of immigration from Scotland throughout the seventeenth century. Three main phases of immigration took place; the Plantation of Ulster[2] by James VI, the 1640s, and the post-Restoration period. This was supplemented by a further wave in the 1690s following harvest failure and the 'Lean Years in Scotland'.[3] By the time of the 1641 Ulster Rising, at least 20,000 Scots and possibly 30,000 had migrated to Ulster from Scotland.[4] One contemporary seventeenth-century commentator, William Petty, observed that by 1672 around 80, 000 'new Scots' had settled in Ireland,[5] although it is now generally accepted that these figures are somewhat exaggerated.[6] It has been estimated that c.10,000 further Scots migrated to Ulster between the Restoration and the Revolution of 1688, with a further 40,000-70,000 Scots crossing to Ulster in the 1690s. Over the period 1650-1700 as a whole, it has been estimated that 60,000-100,000 Scots moved to Ulster.[7] What is clearly the case is that by the late seventeenth century Ulster was a crucial part of the Scottish diaspora.

---

1 For a discussion on Orangeism see E. McFarland, *Protestants first. Orangeism in nineteenth century Scotland* (Edinburgh, 1990). 2 See M. Perceval-Maxwell, *The Scottish migration to Ulster in the reign of James I* (London, 1973). 3 J. Agnew, *Belfast merchant families in the seventeenth century* (Dublin, 1996), p. 70. 4 T.C. Smout, N.C. Landsman, & T.M. Devine, 'Scottish emigration in the seventeenth and eighteenth centuries', in N. Canny (ed.), *Europeans on the move. Studies on European migration 1500-1800* (Cambridge, 1994), p. 78. 5 William Petty, *The political anatomy of Ireland* (London, 1691), quoted in J.G. Simms, *Jacobite Ireland 1685-91* (London, 1969, repr. Dublin, 2000), p. 11. 6 I. McBride, *The siege of Derry in Ulster Protestant mythology* (Dublin, 1997), p. 23. 7 Smout, Landsman & Devine, 'Scottish emigration . . .', pp 87-8.

THE STRATEGIC RESPONSE OF THE 1689
CONVENTION AND PARLIAMENT OF 1689-90

The institutional format of the Williamite regime for the years 1689-90 was based on the 1689 Convention of Estates, which sat from 14 March to 24 May 1689, and then three parliamentary sessions from 5 June 1689 to 10 September 1690.[8] The two other main organs of the administration in Scotland were the Scottish privy council and the general assembly of the Church of Scotland. Whilst Jacobitism initially presented a substantial political threat in the 1689 convention, this was effectively neutralised by the superior political management of the Williamite faction, aided by the sheer political folly of James VII as king of Scotland and his condescending attitude towards the convention. James's letter to the convention referred to 'the infamy and disgrace you bring upon your selves in the world, and the condemnation due to the rebellious in the next' and threatened to 'punish with the rigour of our laws all such as stand in rebellion against us of our authority'.[9] Such an attitude did much to lose James political support in the convention at a time when the Williamite supremacy had still not been secured. Indeed, it was observed that James' letter was 'written in the terms of a conqueror and a priest'.[10] Many of James' supporters withdrew from the convention for their own safety and the 'whig-party, thus left to themselves, proceeded to settle the government'.[11] Factional supremacy was achieved via a Whig majority on the Committee for Controverted Elections.[12] The Scottish Constitutional Settlement enacted in 1689-90 stated that James VII had forfeited his throne as king of Scots and replaced him with William and Mary, whilst the Presbyterian supremacy in the Church of Scotland was also guaranteed.[13]

The strategic response of the new Scottish administration to the war in Ireland was viewed as an integral part of the overall security of the regime. As such, it was viewed in conjunction with the internal threat of Jacobitism and the fear of a Franco-Irish military invasion.[14] The memory of the success of

8 *The Acts of the Parliaments of Scotland* [hereafter, *APS*], (*1689-1695*), ed. T. Thomson (Edinburgh, 1822), pp 3-95, 95-106, 106-230, 232-8. Sessions of this parliament continued to 1702. The parliament of 1689-1702 had 10 sessions in all. 9 D. Szechi, *The Jacobites. Britain and Europe 1688-1788* (Manchester, 1994), pp 140-1. Szechi prints James' letter in full, in the form of 'James II to the Scottish Convention'. This should read as James VII as king of Scotland, as opposed to James II as king of England. 10 Sir J. Dalrymple, *Memoirs of Great Britain and Ireland. From the dissolution of the last parliament of Charles II until the sea-battle off La Hogue*, two volumes, second edition (London, 1821-3), vol. 1, p. 285. 11 Ibid., vol. 1, p. 288. 12 Ibid., p. 284; R.S. Rait, *The Parliaments of Scotland* (Glasgow, 1924), pp 95-6. 13 See I.B. Cowan, 'Church and state reformed ? The revolution of 1688-9 in Scotland', in J. Israel (ed.), *The Anglo-Dutch moment. Essays on the Glorious Revolution and its world impact* (Cambridge, 1991), pp 163-183. 14 *An account of the proceedings of the estates of Scotland 1689-1690*, ed. E.W.M. Balfour-Melville, two volumes (Edinburgh, 1954-1955), vol. 1, pp. 10-11; *The register of the privy*

the devastating campaigns of James Graham, fifth earl and first marquis of Montrose, in Scotland, allied with an Irish Catholic military force in the 1640s, provided a model which the new regime did not wish to see repeated. Contingency plans were formulated within a short time of the meeting of the convention on 14 March 1689.

One of the first strategic decisions taken by the 1689 convention on a national basis was to establish a Committee for Securing the Peace on 16 March with the remit to 'Consider what is fitt to be proposed for secureing of the peace'.[15] The committee reported back to the convention with a six-point agenda on 18 March, although there was no direct mention of Ireland. At this stage, securing Edinburgh, the capital, took priority in the midst of the activities of John Graham of Claverhouse, Viscount Dundee (declared a rebel on 30 March after which he resorted to guerrilla warfare) and the Catholic duke of Gordon (in control of Edinburgh Castle).[16] Considerations of overall national security were therefore legislated for in the Act for putting the Kingdom in a posture of defence of 19 March. All Protestants between the ages of 16 and 60 were ordered to 'be in readiness' with their best horses and ammunition and were to await further instructions from the Estates.[17]

A defining moment for the 1689 convention in the perception of and response to the fate of the Irish Protestants was that of 18 March. William Douglas, third duke of Hamilton, in the capacity of president of the convention,[18] produced a letter 'brought by one Mr Knox from Ireland' which was directed to the attention of the Convention.[19] The letter pleaded for 'christain and neighbourly assisstance to preserve us from mercyles adversaries who are reddie and able to Destroy us'.[20] The letter further informed the convention that the 'wholl power of this kingdom both civill and military is for the most pairt in papist hands' along with garrisons, places of strength and stores and 'wherever the garisones are they prey upon the Brittish and Protestants round about them'.[21] The convention was also informed that the opposing forces in Ireland consisted 'at least of 50,000 men', that Protestant families were in fear of their safety and that the 'protestant partie' was left in 'a manner wholly destitute of armes and amunition' because they had been seized by the opposing forces.[22] The letter also mentioned that Richard Talbot, earl of Tyrconnell, was pressing the earl of Antrim 'to make use of his interest in

council of Scotland [hereafter, *RPCS*], third series, vol. 15, 1690, ed. E.W. M. Balfour-Melville (Edinburgh, 1967), p.14; G. Holmes, *The making of a great power. Late Stuart and early Georgian Britain 1660-1722* (London, 1993), p. 230. **15** *APS*, IX, 10. **16** Ibid. 10-11. The Committee for Securing the Peace was commissioned to continue its activities on 21 May (ibid., 85). **17** Ibid. 13. **18** Hamilton was elected as president of the convention on 14 March (ibid., 6). He secured victory over his rival John Murray, second earl of Atholl, a Jacobite, by a majority of 40 among 150 votes; Cowan, 'Church and state reformed ?', p. 164; Dalrymple, *Memoirs of Great Britain and Ireland*, vol. 1, pp 284-5. **19** *APS*, IX, 12. **20** Ibid. **21** Ibid. **22** Ibid.

the highlands of Scotland' to send over 1500 men to 'assist the popish pairty to reduce the north of Ireland'.[23] The letter therefore asked for firearms and ammunition to be sent over from Scotland to Ireland to aid their cause, which would be interpreted as a 'charitable peace of kyndnes done to your Protestant neighbours in great distress'.[24]

The response of the convention to the Irish letter was immediate and a specialised session committee was established on 18 March 'to meet and consider the condition of the highlands and to report'.[25] It was staffed by Highland magnates and shire and burgh representatives from the Highlands and neighbouring Lowland areas. Hence, Sir James Smollett of Stainflett and Bonhill (Dumbarton), John Cuthbert of Draikes (Inverness) and Hugh Brown (Inverary) were the burgess representatives: their areas of representation were all key strategic locations for the defence of the Highlands as well as the gateway to the Lowlands. In similar fashion, Duncan Forbes of Culloden (Inverness), a hardline Presbyterian,[26] Ludovic Grant of that ilk and of Freuchie (Inverness) and Sir Thomas Burnet of Leys (Kincardine) were amongst the shire representatives on the committee.[27] A Proclamation against Papists was issued on 20 March with three main provisions. Firstly, all Catholics were discharged from holding any civil or military office. Secondly, all Catholics were to surrender their arms, albeit 'gentlemen' were allowed to keep their 'ordinary wearing swords'! Thirdly, all Catholics who did not belong to Edinburgh or areas nearby were required to withdraw from the capital to places at least 10 miles away or to their homes within 48 hours.[28]

A further series of strategic and logistical decisions were taken on 21 and 22 March. The duke of Hamilton, as president of the convention, was empowered by the Estates to 'dispatch persones as he shall see cause to the Kingdome of Ireland towards Belfast, Londonderry or elswher for getting intelligence.'[29] The inclusion of Sir James Smollett, burgess representative for Dumbarton, on the committee anent the condition of the Highlands, was complemented by instructions given to Major George Arnot, lieutenant governor of the garrison of Dumbarton Castle, to report to the convention with details of stores, ammunition and the overall condition of the garrison.[30] A further committee was established on 21 March and it was instructed to enquire on the state of 'the publick armes'. The south-west of Scotland secured particular representation via shire and burgh commissioners; William Blair of that ilk (Ayr) and Sir Andrew Agnew of Lochnaw (Wigtown) for the shires, with John Muir (Ayr) as one of the burgess representatives.[31] Measures were also taken to defend and arm the west and south-west coast of Scotland, because of their proximity to

23 Ibid.   24 Ibid. The letter mentioned that similar appeals for military support were also being made to England. 25 Ibid.   26 Ibid. 27 Ibid. 28 Ibid. 16. 29 Ibid. 17. 30 Ibid. 31 Ibid.

the Irish sea. The Act for Distribution of Arms among the Western Shires provided for the distribution of arms for Glasgow, Paisley, Ayr, Kirkcudbright, Stranraer and Inverary. Ammuntions were also ordered to be transferred from Stirling Castle for storage in Glasgow Tolbooth for the defence of Glasgow and the western counties.[32] Fifteen hundred muskets, 30 chests of ball, and 500 pikes were later delivered to John Muir, provost of Ayr, for the defence of Ayrshire.[33]

The Williamite administration in Scotland moved quickly to control and monitor the movement of population between Scotland and Ireland via the Act for Securing Suspected Persons of 22 March.[34] Guards were to be strengthened at seaports, bridges, ferries and other places of passage.[35] Western ports were ordered to 'stop and secure all persons going to Ireland without Passes, till they give a good account of their business'.[36] Attempted control of the sea traffic between Scotland and Ireland was continued via a parliamentary embargo of 16 April which proscribed any sailings to Ireland. This was justified because of the potential dangers of 'allowing ships and other vessells liberty to pass from this Kingdome to Ireland In regaird they be made use of in the case of ane invasion for transporting forces hither'.[37]

A fundamental element in the strategic calculations of the Williamite regime in Scotland related to the actual theatre and zone of military conflict. Quite simply, a military clash between William and James was to be kept out of Scotland and restricted to Ireland, if at all possible. Troops and supplies were to be sent to Ireland, certainly as part of helping the cause of the Irish Protestants, but also as a way of keeping that military conflict out of Scotland. Indeed, such a strategy was articulated at an early stage in the life of the new

---

32 Ibid., 18, 20-21. A parliamentary warrant was also issued on 22 March for drawing together the 'fencible men' in Glasgow, whilst further legislation was enacted on 2 April for transporting arms to Glasgow. That the Highland dimension was also foremost in the regime's mind was reflected in legislation of 2 April for providing the magistrates of Inverness with ammunition (ibid., 21-2, 31-2, 32-3). See also *Accounts of the proceedings of the estates*, vol. 1, pp 9, 16. 33 James Paterson, *History of the counties of Ayr and Wigton* (Edinburgh, 1863), vol. 1, Kyle, Part I, ccvi. Provost John Muir later claimed £130 Scots in expenses from the government as due payment for intelligence reports on Ireland; M. Young (ed.), *The parliaments of Scotland. Burgh and shire commissioners*, two volumes (Edinburgh, 1992-93), vol. 2, p. 514. 34 *APS*, IX, 19. The duke of Hamilton, as president of the convention, received authorisation on 8 April to secure 'any suspect persones untill they find Cautione for keeping the peace'. This warrant was to be based on any information that Hamilton may have on suspects. Hamilton was also authorised to bring in English forces to secure the border if he thought that such action was required: ibid., 35. 35 *Accounts of the proceedings of the estates*, vol. 1, p. 16. 36 Ibid., pp 23-4. 37 *APS*, IX, 45-6. Legislation was enacted in favour of several merchants from Belfast and Derry on 13 April. Ships which had sailed from Derry and Belfast and docked at Ayr, Saltcoats and other places in the Clyde. They had brought women and children escaping the troubles as well as goods to support the refugee families in Scotland. Parliamentary legislation allowed the ships to return to Derry for 'disburthening' of Derry (and other places) of women and children (*APS*, IX, 44-5).

regime in Scotland. On 23 March 1689 Sir John Dalrymple of Stair, a central
figure of the new regime, informed George, earl of Melville, secretary of state,
that 10,000 men might be raised in Scotland and that this 'might be the neirest
way to releive our freinds in Ireland, at least to save invasione on Brittan, which
will certainly be on Scotland rather then on England.'[38] Four days later, on 27
March, Dalrymple informed Melville from London that he had told William
of Orange that 'the Scots would quicklie be ready, and would cheirfully goe to
save ther brethern in Irland, and meet the Irish ther, rather then wait for them
at home.'[39] By 5 April Dalrymple was demanding that military forces be sent
to Londonderry; 'I sie no appearance of safty of our cuntry if ther be not an
armie sent to Dary, able to take the field.'[40] The point that Dalrymple was driving home was precise: 'It is far safer to deall with enemies in ther owne cuntry
then in ours, wher a concurs may be to ther assistance.'[41] This was a clear reference to the destabilising effects of internal insurrection, especially in the
form of Jacobitism. William of Orange, in correspondence with Hamilton,
himself recognised that measures were necessary 'for preventing your countrey' from becoming 'the seatt of warr and thereby may become a field of
blood'.[42]

Fears of an Irish invasion accelerated in April 1689. Francis Brady, a
Jacobite spy, was captured at Greenock having returned to Scotland from
Dublin. Brady had left Scotland on 6 March and he was captured with a series
of devastating letters from James and his henchman John Drummond, first
earl of Melfort, to several of their key supporters in Scotland; Colin Lindsay,
third earl of Balcarres, Viscount Dundee and Melfort's brother, James
Drummond, fourth earl of Perth (in common with Melfort, he was also a
recent Catholic convert). These letters suggested that James had 40-50 000
men in Ireland and that Dundee should call a rival convention to defend
James's cause. Not only did this accelerate fears of an Irish invasion of Scotland,
but also of a political coup d'etat through a rival Jacobite convention.[43]

---

38 *Leven and Melville papers. Letters and state papers chiefly addressed to George earl of Melville,
secretary of state for Scotland 1689-91* (Edinburgh, 1843), p. 4.   39 Ibid., p. 5.   40 Ibid., p. 7.
41 Ibid.   42 Historical Manuscripts Commission. *Eleventh report, appendix, part 6. The
manuscripts of the duke of Hamilton* (London, 1887), p. 176.   43 *Accounts of the proceedings of the
estates*, vol. 1, p. 24. Brady was transferred from Greenock to Glasgow before being examined by
the convention in Edinburgh. See also HMC, *Eleventh report, manuscripts of the duke of Hamilton*,
pp 178-9. Legislation was also enacted on 22 April for a military garrison to be provided for the
Castle of Arran, which belonged to the duke of Hamilton himself. Arran Castle was identified as
bein 'a Place of great strenth and Importance in the tyme of warr, and may be of great use to the
Island and Countrey Incaice any Invasione shall happen from Ireland'. Accordingly, a troop of 40
men was to be levied to garrison the castle and Hamilton was appointed captain and commander
of that body (*APS*, IX, 57-58). It appears that James had failed to follow Viscount Dundee's
advice for a military invasion of Scotland to team up with Highland clans, an option that was later
to be regretted after defeat at the Boyne; J. MacKnight (ed.), *Memoirs of Sir Ewen Cameron of*

Melfort's tone demanding retribution for the opponents of James in Scotland was particularly severe and did much to weaken James's cause. It was reported that Melfort had said that 'he will make them Gideonites, hewers of wood and drawers of water for their Catholick Friends the only true Israelites indeed'.[44] Melfort was one of James's closest advisors and had landed with James in Kinsale, County Cork, also accompanied by Conrad von Rosen, a lieutenant general of the French army.[45] Contemporary descriptions indicate that Melfort was 'abhorred by the Presbyterians' in Scotland.[46]

A further wave of fear of an Irish invasion emerged in June and July 1689. General Hugh Mackay of Scourie, commander of William's forces in Scotland, in correspondence with Hamilton, was particularly scathing that he had learned 'with wonder of an invasion from Ireland', in his correspondence with Hamilton,[47] because such an eventuality should have been prevented by coastal controls. Correspondence from Archibald Campbell, tenth earl of Argyll to Hamilton in mid-July heightened these fears. Argyll had arrived in Dumbarton by 14 July where he 'had been assured' that the 'Irish also design an invasion of England', as well as forces linking up with Dundee at Inverlochy (present-day Fort William).[48] The overall logic of this Jacobite strategy emanating from Ireland, as perceived by Argyll, was 'certainle to make a diversion' in the Highlands 'whilst about the same tyme they invade England'.[49] Intelligence information received from Campbeltown and Inverary also indicated French naval activity near Jura and Islay.[50] Such information was complemented by other intelligence sources. On 18 July 1689 it was noted that 'some hundreds of Irish Papists' had been shipped at Carrickfergus to join Viscount Dundee in Scotland.[51] Two days later, on 20 July, parliament was informed that Sir Duncan Campbell of Auchinbreck had captured three boats full of Irish, who were to be transported from Argyllshire to Edinburgh, and that the estimate of the numbers of Irish who had landed was put at 500 men.[52] Further reports suggested that 400 Irish had landed in Mull and that Dundee was 'endeavouring all he can to draw all the Clans together to joyn him, which with those Irish, may make a body of several Hundreds of men'.[53] This was a particularly crucial time given the Jacobite victory at Killiecrankie, albeit its importance was lessened by the death of Dundee in active combat.[54]

Locheill, chief of the clan Cameron (Edinburgh, 1842), pp 296-7; Dalrymple, *Memoirs of Great Britain and Ireland*, vol. 1, pp 286-7.   **44** *Account of the proceedings of the estates*, vol. 1, p. 47. **45** J.G. Simms, 'The war of the two kings 1685-91', in T.W. Moody, F.X. Martin & F.J. Byrne (eds), *A new history of Ireland*. vol. 3. *Early modern Ireland, 1534-1691* (Oxford, 1976), p. 485. **46** Dalrymple, *Memoirs of Great Britain and Ireland*, vol. 1, p. 285.   **47** HMC, *Eleventh report, Hamilton manuscripts*, p. 179.   **48** Ibid., p. 182.   **49** Ibid.   **50** Ibid.   **51** *Accounts of the proceedings of the estates*, vol. 1, p. 173.   **52** Ibid., p. 175.   **53** Ibid., p. 179.   **54** The rebellion was effectively ended by the defence of Dunkeld by Cameronians on 21 August. Fears of further Jacobite resistance continued from 1689-91, however, especially if there was an invasion from Ireland; Cowan, 'Church and State reformed ?', p. 165.

The co-ordination of intelligence reports clearly formed an important aspect of the decision-making process for the Williamite regime based In Edinburgh. Three main categories of intelligence reports can be identified for the period 1689-90. Firstly, coastal activity and shipping were monitored, especially in terms of Franco-Irish activity and potential threats of invasion. On 21 March 1689 the convention allocated two small frigates 'to Cruise betwixt Scotland and Ireland' for the purpose of producing intelligence reports.[55] Captain William Hamilton and a Captain John Brown were commissioned as commanders of the two frigates. Hamilton, in particular, was commissioned to sail out of the River Clyde and cruise the west coast from the point of Cornwall to the Isle of Skye. He was also authorised to fight, apprehend and sink if necessary, any ships of King James 'or any persones under his Command'.[56] Likewise, he was authorised to seize any individuals, goods, arms or horses pertaining to the use or defence of James.[57] In early May 1690 a vessel by the name of *Swiftsure* had been captured, its crew was imprisoned and Jacobite agents aboard seized.[58] Seizure was not restricted to suspicious vessels or activities; the *Jean and Katherine of Dublin* were seized by an English captain, depite the fact that they were trading legally between Dublin and Glasgow.[59]

The second main category of reports were concerned with the Siege of Londonderry itself. Thus, in May 1689 it was noted that 'From Ireland we hear, That London-derry defends itself bravely.'[60] In terms of overall Scottish strategic security, it was observed on 15 June 1689 with regard to Londonderry that 'the Preservation of those Brave People and Town' was of 'great Importance'.[61] Concern for the welfare of the inhabitants of Londonderry continued in the period after the relief of the siege. In October 1689, for example, it was noted that the 'Inhabitants of that Town are beginning to recover their Health, after much Sickness and Indisposition of Body'.[62] Thirdly, regular reports were provided on the general progress of the Williamite war in Ireland. First-hand reports were often taken from refugees who had escaped from Ireland. Hence, one 'Mr Bennett' who had escaped from Derry, was interviewed in April 1689 by the earl of Lothian and Sir Patrick Home of Polwarth,[63] in the form of an official delegation from the convention, on the

55 *Account of the proceedings of the estates*, vol. 1, p. 10. See also (*APS*, IX, 17). Letters written on 8 May by Captain Hamilton confirmed that he had taken and destroyed 'some Boats belonging to the Enemy on the Irish coast' (*Accounts of the proceedings of the estates*, vol. 1, p. 90). A small boat was also kept at Portpatrick 'to facilitate rapid communication with Ireland; *RPCS*, third series, vol. 14, 1689, ed. H. Paton (Edinburgh, 1933), p. 22. 56 *APS*, IX, 44-45. 57 Ibid. 58 *RPCS*, third series, vol. 15, 1690, ed. E.W.M. Balfour-Melville (Edinburgh, 1967), p. 14. 59 Ibid. 60 *Accounts of the proceedings of the estates*, vol. 1, p. 106. 61 Ibid., p. 132. 62 Ibid., vol. 2, p. 39. 63 Sir Patrick Home of Polwarth was one of the leading Presbyterians who had been in exile in Holland and had accompanied William of Orange to England. He had fled to Holland after been implicated in the Rye House plot of 1683 and he had also taken part in the abortive Argyll rebellion of 1685. Home of Polwarth was a leading player in the new Presbyterian

issue of condition of Derry. Bennett was also being asked for information concerning the condition of Ireland.[64] On 14 June 1689 reports received from Kyntre based on information from Irish refugees specified that Ireland was in a 'miserable condition; and that they believe that the Protestants and Papists there will want Bread within a little time, all people expecting a Famine there'.[65] The records of the Scottish privy council also indicate the logistical importance of troop movements and provisioning throughout 1690 between Scotland and Ulster. Provisions were supplied from Glasgow to Belfast.[66] Treasury orders in April 1690 instructed the town council of Glasgow to arrange for two ships to be provided for the transportation of 600 soldiers with provisions.[67] Danish troops under the duke of Schomberg's command were to march from Leith to the south-west where they were to sail from Kirkcudbright to the theatre of war in Ireland. Several small boats were also provided in early July 1690 to keep the privy council informed of the progress of the Williamite campaign.[68]

TALES OF ATROCITIES INFLICTED ON PROTESTANT SETTLERS IN ULSTER

The Jacobite War in Ireland and the fate of the Irish Protestants reactivated fears of a repeat of the massacres of 1641. Stories and reports of the massacre of innocent Protestants flooded back to Scotland throughout 1689–90.[69] The exposure of the Comber Letter of December 1688 in Ulster bred widespread fear and panic amongst Ulster Protestants of mass slaughter of their kin and co-religionists.[70] Yet, from a Scottish perspective, it was also noted that a custom had prevailed, 'almost habitual to the Irish Protestants, of seeing Irish massacres in imagination'.[71] Thus, on 11 May 1689 the convention was informed of the murder of Protestants near Londonderry who had sought

regime. He represented Berwickshire in the 1689 convention and then in the parliament of 1689–90. As well as being a Scottish privy councillor, he was raised to the peerage as Lord Polwarth in 1690, before later becoming earl of Marchmont in 1702: M. Young (ed.), *The parliaments of Scotland*, vol. 1, pp 353–4. **64** *Account of the proceedings of the estates*, vol. 1, pp 75–8. **65** Ibid., p. 126. **66** *RPCS*, 1690, xiv. **67** *Extracts from the records of the Burgh of Glasgow A.D. 1663–1690*, ed. J.D. Marwick (Glasgow, 1905), pp 447–8. The execution of these orders was delegated to John Anderson, provost of Glasgow, who subsequently arranged for the provision of two ships via two Glasgow merchants, William Walkinshaw and Thomas Peter. **68** *RPCS*, 1690, xiv. **69** James B. Woodburn, an early twentieth-century writer, argued that in the years 1689–91 in Ireland 'there were no such atrocities committed as those which disgraced 1641': Woodburn, *The Ulster Scot. His history and religion* (London, 1914), p. 171. **70** A.T.Q. Stewart, *The narrow ground. Aspects of Ulster 1609–1969* (London, 1977), pp 64–5; J.G. Simms, p. 49. **71** Dalrymple, *Memoirs of Great Britain and Ireland*, vol. 1, p. 292. For a recent reassessment of the scale of atrocities committed in 1641, see N. Canny, 'What really happened in Ireland in

protection from the king. The fate of one Ensign Thompson was highlighted. Thompson had invited Irish and French officers to a 'feast', seeking the protection of James, and pleaded with them, 'as Gentlemen and Soldiers, to preserve him and his family'.[72] Despite guarantees of his safety, however, Thompson and his family were murdered later in the evening. The official records of the Scottish convention, in response to this news, clearly noted that 'Such examples are too plentiful in every corner of that poor country'.[73] Tales of suffering and persecution were often brought over by refugees to Scotland. The convention was informed on 28 May 1689 by one (unidentified) refugee who had escaped from Killyheagh that 'the Irish have been barbarously cruel there'.[74] In particular, four elderly gently men were slaughtered, as were twelve women, five of whom were pregnant. The latter were killed 'because they bred Hereticks'[75] (that is, Protestants). Tales of Protestant suffering also extended to Dublin and Cork. A 'melancholy account' was given to parliament on 1 October 1689 by 'one lately come from Dublin' in which the state of the Protestants in the Dublin area was commented on.[76] According to this report, new prisons were being created and Protestants were being imprisoned immediately on their discovery. Moreover, it was claimed that the vaults and cellars under such prisons were being filled with gunpowder, a fact which heightened 'the dismal apprehensions of those unfortunate people, to be either Blown up, or have their Throats cut'.[77] On 12 November the unfortunate fate of one Mr Rutter, the keeper of the Garter Tavern in Dublin, was noted by parliament. Rutter had been serving wine to French and Irish officers in his tavern, but had refused to join them in a toast which pledged 'Confusion to all the English, and Hereticks in general'.[78] Despite Rutter's polite insistence that he could not join them on the grounds that he was a Protestant, 'no excuse would save him from their fury', and after being called a 'Heretical Dog', he was executed on the spot by one of the officers.[79] In January 1690 a ship arrived from Cork and news filtered out that 'most of the Protestant Inhabitants of Cork are turned out of the Gates',[80] whilst in Febuary 1690 letters received from Belfast indicated that in Munster and Leinster the 'popish clergy . . . did invade most of the Churches in the Protestant hands in those Provinces, and expell'd all the Protestants from them'.[81]

Reports of such atrocities inflicted on the Protestant settlers were of profound importance to the impact and perception of the native Scottish Protestant psyche, irrespective of their historical accuracy. Contemporaries clearly believed that such tales were true and they reacted accordingly in terms

1641 ?', in Jane H. Ohlmeyer (ed.), *Ireland from independence to occupation 1641–1660* (Cambridge, 1995), pp 24-42. **72** *Accounts of the proceedings of the estates*, volume 1, p. 84. **73** Ibid. **74** Ibid., p. 107. **75** Ibid. **76** Ibid., vol. 2, p. 25. **77** Ibid. **78** Ibid., p. 55. **79** Ibid. **80** Ibid., p. 99. **81** Ibid., p. 108.

of the decision-making process and policy options. The memory of 1641 remained a real one and the Ulster settlers were regarded as the brethren of the Scots. A clear historical link can therefore be made between the perceptions of and reactions to the Ulster massacres of 1641 and the events of 1689-90 in Ireland. The legacy of 1641 was profound for the course of the seventeenth century as a whole within a British context. As Jane Ohlmeyer has recently noted, 'many Protestants viewed the conflict as a religious struggle. The Ulster rebellion confirmed and inflamed fears that a great Catholic conspiracy was about to engulf Britain and reduce it to popery.'[82] Such fears clearly reverberated once more in 1689-90.

ETHNICITY AND THE RESPONSE OF WILLIAMITE ESTABLISHMENT IN SCOTLAND

On 18 April the convention legislated in favour of 'the British Protestants comed from Ireland'. This legislation was based on a petition submitted by James Stewart, a Belfast merchant, on behalf of the 'British Protestants in the Kingdome of Ireland'.[83] Stewart's petition was based directly on the situation in Derry whereby

> That by reason of the prevailing of the Irish in Ireland ther are several thousands of the British Protestants come together about Derry who can neither be admitted into the toun of Derry, because they wold increase ther numbers, above what condition of the place can bear, nor are they able to keep the fields, against the strong power of the Irish papists threatning to come against them, so that they are in hazard to be exposed to their crueltie and rage.[84]

The fate of the Protestants massed in Derry was weakened by the current embargo on ships between Scotland and Ireland. Stewart claimed that such Protestants would be willing and ready to 'engage in his Majesties service for the Defence of this Kingdome'[85] (that is, Scotland). Stewart petitioned for ships to be allowed to sail for Derry or the most safe and convenient ports for the cause. Many of the ships in question were actually owned by the petitioners, thereby reducing the burden on the new Scottish administration, and it does appear that the British Protestant petitioners wished to return to Ireland to fight their cause. Having been considered by the Committee for Securing the Peace of the Kingdom, the petition was granted and the embargo on the

---

82 Jane H. Ohlmeyer, 'The Wars of Religion', in T. Bartlett & K. Jeffrey (eds), *A military history of Ireland* (Cambridge, 1996), p. 186. 83 *APS*, IX, 49. 84 Ibid. 85 Ibid.

western ports of Scotland was lifted in terms of communication with Ireland. A Scottish convoy was ordered to escort the Irish vessels to and from Ireland.[86]

Close ethnic, family and trading links had been strongly established between Scotland and Ulster throughout the seventeenth century and such links were further activated when Ireland became destabilised in 1689. Coleraine, Londonderry and Carrickfergus each had large populations of Scottish Presbyterians, whilst the Belfast merchant community was dominated by an oligarchy of a Scottish trading mafia.[87] Indeed, Belfast itself was seen primarily as Scots town,[88] whilst it has been estimated that the majority of the defenders at Londonderry were Scots Presbyterians.[89] One contemporary commentator described the defenders of Londonderry as being 'possessed of the valour and enthusiasm of those Scottish ancestors from whom most of the inhabitants of Ulster are descended'.[90] In 1689 most of the Belfast burgesses who were of Scottish origin returned to Scotland and many were located in Glasgow and south-west Scotland in 1689, especially the town of Ayr. William Crawford, MP for Belfast 1703-13, a Presbyterian of Scottish origin and a founder member of the second Belfast Congregation, fled to Glasgow in 1689, George Brown McCartney, a Presbyterian merchant and shipowner of Belfast, fled to Ayr and stayed there 1689-90, whilst John Black, another Presbyterian Belfast merchant, also fled to Ayr with his family in 1689.[91]

The majority of Belfast merchants aligned themselves politically with the Williamite cause in the clash with James VII and II.[92] This alignment and support was reflected in direct action and material support from those with Scottish links and origins, albeit from the relative safety of the Scottish mainland. Henry Clads had been active in the Belfast militia and had provided them

---

86 Ibid.   87 Jean Agnew, *Belfast merchant families*, p. 10. Agnew's study was based on 32 Belfast merchant families. 'At least twenty-two were of Scottish origin, including direct immigrants from Scotland and descendants of Scottish families already settled in Ulster'.   88 Ibid., p. 26. The majority of Scots who settled in Belfast were from south-west Scotland (Ibid., 65).   89 R. Bagwell, *Ireland under the Stuarts and during the Interregnum*, vol. 3, 1660-1690 (London, 1916), p. 241.   90 Dalrymple, *Memoirs of Great Britain and Ireland*, vol. 1, p. 329. One early twentieth-century commentator observed that 'among the officers the English and the Scots were nearly equal, but at least nine-tenths of the citizens and of the garrison were Scots': Woodburn, *The Ulster Scot. His history and religion*, p. 155.   91 Agnew, *Belfast merchant families*, pp 211-12, 219-220, 245-6. It was also observed that 'Many of the rich, and of the weaker sex removed their persons and their effects to strong places, and into Scotland and England' (Dalrymple, *Memoirs of Great Britain and Ireland*, vol. 1, pp 296-7). Dalrymple's comments here relate to the organisation of Protestant resistance in the form of the Northern Associations on the one hand and temporary/permanent migration to Scotland and England on the other. From a more general point of view, the Williamite regime passed legislation on 16 August 1689, following the arrival of Schomberg in Ireland, which allowed Irish Protestant refugees to return home. This might well suggest that the regime was wary of being overburdened with Irish Protestants on a permanent basis; *Account of the proceedings of the estates*, vol. 2, p. 12.   92 Agnew, *Belfast merchant families*, p. 88.

with arms in 1689, before escaping to Ayr, and he can be traced to Glasgow in June 1689.[93] Colonel Edward Brice, a Presbyterian merchant and shipowner in Belfast and Kilroot, not only escaped to Scotland but he also raised a regiment which fought in the Jacobite Wars.[94] Indeed, the Scottish parliament/convention legislated in favour of Bryce and the 'Irish Protestants' on 2 April 1689 to allow Bryce to convene his company of troops at Greenock.[95]

In many respects, the North Channel link between Scotland and Ulster was personified by George McCartney of Auchinleck and Thomas Knox. Both had strong Scottish links, albeit both were members of the Church of Ireland. McCartney had been born in Auchinleck in 1626 before migrating to Belfast in 1649 where he advanced to high office, including that of surveyor-general of the customs of Ulster in 1683. As well as being a merchant and shipowner in Belfast, McCartney supplied revenue to the Protestant Northern Association and was captain of a troop of horse which was first to proclaim William and Mary in Ireland. He had returned to Scotland with his wife and family by April 1689, after his property had been seized.[96] McCartney has been described by Louis Cullen as 'the greatest Belfast merchant of the day'.[97] The close internal cohesion of the dominant Scottish group within the Belfast merchant community was also reflected in the close family links between McCartney and another Protestant refugee who fled to Scotland (Glasgow) in 1689, namely one William Lockhart. Lockhart was of Scottish origin, possibly a second generation migrant, and was a merchant and shipowner in Belfast. Lockhart's wife was the daughter of George McCartney of Auchinleck.[98] Thomas Knox, a merchant of Belfast and Dungannon, also returned to the land of his birth in 1689 when he fled to Glasgow. Knox had been created a burgess of Belfast in 1680 as well as a burgess of Glasgow in 1686 and subsequently was the MP for Newtoun in 1692-3 and Dungannon on an intermittent basis from 1695-1727.[99] It would also appear that he was the 'Mr Knox' who delivered the letter to the 1689 Convention on the condition of the Irish Protestants.

Robert Lennox, a merchant and shipowner of Belfast, had close links with Londonderry. Lennox had jointly petitioned the Scottish Privy Council with one Alexander Lecky on 26 July 1689 for a pass to send ships to take provisions to Londonderry. Lennox's own family origins were Scottish and based in Derry and he was also an elder of the first Belfast Presbyterian congregation. His brother, James Lennox, was a merchant and shipowner in Londonderry and a captain of one of the eight companies for the defence of Londonderry.

---

93 Ibid., p. 216. Clads was also a Presbyterian and he was a ruling elder at Befast in 1692, 1698 and 1704. Clads was involved in the sale of arms and ammunition in Glasgow in June 1689 (ibid., p. 89-90). **94** Ibid., p.212-14. Brice later became MP for Dungannon, 1702-13. **95** *APS*, IX, 31. **96** Agnew, *Belfast merchant families*, p. 89, pp 233-8. **97** L.M. Cullen, 'Economic Trends 1660-91', in Moody, Martin & Byrne (eds), *A new history of Ireland*, vol. 3, p. 453. **98** Agnew, *Belfast merchant families*, pp 232-3. **99** Ibid., pp 227-8.

James Lennox later became mayor of Londonderry in 1693 and 1697 and he eventually became the MP for Londonderry borough in the period 1703-13.[100]

VOLUNTARY CONTRIBUTIONS, FINANCIAL
SUPPORT AND HUMANITARIAN AID

On 29 April the convention legislated for Protestant refugees who had fled to Scotland in the Act for the Voluntary Contribution to the Irish and French Protestants. The Estates took to their 'serious consideration' the fact that there were so many Irish and French Protestants who had fled to Scotland 'for shelter and refuige, whose necessitous condition calls for the charitable supply of all good christians'.[101] A specific process was formally laid out by the convention for raising a voluntary contribution on a national basis. Firstly, voluntary contributions were to be collected either at the doors of parish churches or from 'persones at ther privat houses'. Secondly, a specific fifteeen-day time-period was allocated for the collection of such contributions after the call for voluntary contributions was read out in parish churches. The deadline for collection was set for 1 July and a formal intimation for collection was to be made at Edinburgh on 12 May. A geographic and logistical division for collection was also established, based on the river Tay as a dividing line. Parishes which had no ministers at that time were to be dealt with by other ministers of the Presbytery or provincial assembly within which the ministerless parishes were situated. They were also to be aided by 'such of the parochiners as are best qualified for such a Charitable work'.[102] Collections and contributions on a national basis were to be delivered to the moderator of the Presbytery or provincial assembly and then forwarded to Sir Patrick Murray, the general receiver, or one of his deputies.[103] Moreover, collections for French and Irish Protestants were not to be restricted to Presbyterian churches. The privy council established a committee on 27 September 1689 for collection from Episcopal churches.[104]

Widespread deprivations of ministers who refused to conform to the new Presbyterian regime took place throughout the autumn and winter of 1689. Several ministers who refused to read the Proclamation for Voluntary Contributions for French and Irish Protestants in their churches and/or refused to participate in the collection of such contributions were deprived by the privy council. This was not the sole reason for deprivation, but was part and parcel of a tripartite attack which also included failure to publicly pray for King William and Queen Mary and failure to read a proclamation observing a day of thanksgiving and solemn fast and humiliation. Many of these ministers hailed from north-east Scotland, the spiritual and ideological heartland of

100 Ibid., pp 231-2. 101 *APS*, IX, 78. 102 Ibid. 103 Ibid. 104 *RPCS*, 1689, 361.

Jacobitism.[105] A series of deprivations took place in the shire of Elgin in October 1689, including Mr Alexander Todd, minister of Elgin, Mr James Gordon minister at Urquhart and Mr James Strachan, minister at Keith.[106]

The call for voluntary contributions for French and Irish Protestants appears to have received a warm response from the populace at large. This can be illustrated by a case study of the kirk session records of Bunkle and Preston in the presbytery of Haddington.[107] Details of voluntary contributions are recorded in the kirk session records from 26 May 1689 to 4 May 1690.[108] The largest sum raised was that of 26 May 1689 with 38 shillings and eight pennies Scots being advanced for the relief of the Irish and French Protestants 'that have fled to this Kingdom'.[109] Specific individuals who had fled from Ireland to Scotland were often identified. Hence, on 9 June 1689, 12 shillings Scots were given to Andrew Scot and John Strachan, 'two honest men from Ireland'.[110] On 23 June 6 shillings were provided for one William Stewart, 'a distrest gentleman from Ireland with his wife and children'.[111] The concern for Irish Protestant refugees in particular, however, was fundamental to the wider Christian compassion for the welfare of the impoverished within Bunkle and Preston.[112] Thus, on 6 October 1689 17 shillings were given to John Shisolm [Chisholm], 'an old poor man in the parish lying bedrid'.[113] One week later, on 13 October, James Lawder received 12 shillings, Marion Johnstone twenty shillings, Janet Thomson twentie shillings and 'Nicolas Richison' six shillings. All were described as 'being poor people in the parish'.[114]

The Scottish privy council, as a national institution and organ of the Scottish administration, was also petitioned by Irish Protestant refugees for relief. Many of these petitions were from Presbyterian ministers. One John Smith was a minister of Clocher in County Tyrone and had fled to Scotland, leaving his wife and children in Ireland, and now wished to return home. The privy council considered a petition from Smith on 2 July 1690 whereby he stated that he wished to return to his ministry in Ulster but did not wish to return 'empty handed'. Although there was an embargo on the export of victuall from Scotland, Smith petitioned to be allowed to export ten bolls of meal to Londonderry for the personal use of himself and his family and not for profit-making motives. Smith's petition was granted by the privy council.[115] Humanitarian concern was also shown by the privy council earlier on 5 May 1690 in the case of one Barbara McDonald, the widow of a Belfast seaman

105 It has been estimated that 'over half the parish ministers of Scotland were disaffected to the new Presbyterian settlement' in 1690 and that the hard core of Jacobitism lay with the 500-600 Episcopalian clergy; B. Lenman, 'The Scottish episcopal clergy and the ideology of Jacobitism', in E. Cruickshanks (ed.), *Ideology and conspiracy: aspects of Jacobitism, 1689-1759* (Edinburgh, 1982), p. 39. 106 Ibid., pp 405-10, 466-8. 107 James Hardy, *The session book of Bunkle and Preston, 1665-1690* (Alnwick, 1900). 108 Ibid., pp 102-5. 109 Ibid., p. 102. 110 Ibid. 111 Ibid. 112 Ibid., pp 8-9. 113 Ibid., p. 103. 114 Ibid. 115 Ibid., pp 302-3.

named William Hamilton who had been killed in William's service at Carrick-fergus. McDonald was left a widow with three children. She was described as being in a 'very miserable and sterving condition', with no means of support for her children, and had been forced to flee to Scotland 'to seek bread to her cheldrein'.[116] Her petition was backed by a Mr John Hamilton, a minister of Newtoun in Ireland, and now a minister in Cramond. McDonald's petition was referred to the Treasury to decide on the appropriate amount of money which would allow her to return to Ireland.[117]

A series of petitions were considered on 14 August 1690, several of which were related directly to the siege of Londonderry. Henry Carter was described as a 'sometyme citizen in Culrain in Ireland' and had personally suffered during the siege. Carter had survived the siege, but had lost a brother, a sister and a child. Carter's petition pleaded for financial support on the grounds that he had a wife and two children, one of whom was only five weeks old, and that he was unable to provide for his family as he could not work because of the suffering he had been inflicted with during the siege itself. The council reacted in a sympathetic manner and remitted his case to the Treasury Commissioners to provide Carter with an appropriate amount.[118] A similar petition was received from Catherine Bruce, whose husband, James Cuthbertson, had been killed at the siege. Cuthbertson was an Irish sea merchant and his death left his wife to raise four children. Having fled to Scotland, Bruce had no means of support and wished to travel south to England where she and her children would be supported by friends. Bruce had no means to finance the journey and her case was remitted to the Treasury to provide a charitable amount to finance this.[119] Richard 'Lowis' (Lewis), a settler in Ulster, had risen in arms for the Williamite cause in Ireland, but had failed to secure entry to Londonderry when many of the Protestant settler community flocked there in panic. Lewis thus fled to Scotland where he was interned in the earl of Glencairn's regiment and held the office of lieutenant. He now wished to return to Ireland but was due seven months arrears of pay and was currently penniless with no personal connections in Scotland. The Treasury Commissioners were therefore instructed to pay Lewis an amount compensate to the office of lieutenant.[120]

Presbyterian ministers from Ulster were particularly active in petitioning the privy council for financial support and ecclesiastical office. The privy council established a general principle concerning Presbyterian ministers who had fled from Ireland and had since taken up the ministry of vacant parishes in Scotland. Several (unidentified) presbyteries in the west of Scotland were described in the Act in favour of the Presbyterian ministers of 11 July 1690 as having 'unfixed ministers (for the most part fledd out of Ireland)'.[121] Such

---

116 Ibid., p. 227.   117 Ibid.   118 Ibid, p. 385.   119 Ibid.   120 Ibid., p. 386.   121 Ibid., xiv, p. 316. The act itself was not primarily concerned with Presbyterian ministers from Ireland, but it did mention their situation.

ministers were allowed to take up the vacant stipends of those parishes in which they had located themselves, albeit they had to be approved by the local Presbytery 'upon productione of certificats testifieing their service'.[122]

THE WILLIAMITE VICTORY IN IRELAND AND SCOTTISH PROTESTANT CELEBRATIONS

> Where-ever he appears, all persons do no less admire his Modesty now, then they did before his Courage, Conduct, and Success in the Preservation of Londonderry.[123]

George Walker, 'the Brave and Worthy Governour of Londonderry', was described in such flattering terms following his appearance in Edinburgh in August 1689. Walker was received in the Scottish capital as a champion of Protestantism and the embodiment of the spirit of Londonderry which had overcome the forces of adversity. Walker was rewarded with the freedom of Glasgow and Edinburgh and Edinburgh also provided him with a 'publick Entertainment'.[124] In terms of two of the traditional icons of modern Ulster Protestant identity, however, it was news of King William's victory at the battle of the Boyne which was accorded greater importance and celebration in Scotland.

News of William's victory at the Boyne was gratefully received by the Scottish parliament. The earl of Crawford, president of parliament, gave an account of the battle to parliament and an order was given for the privy council to appoint 'ane solemne day of thanksgiveing for the forsaid great victory'.[125] A monthly fast was also to be held for the continuation of the war in Ireland against the enemies of King William.[126] An extraordinary meeting of the privy council was held on the same day as parliament had been informed of the victory. Melville, his majesty's high commissioner, informed the council of the 'joyfull and happie newes of the totall defeat of the forces of the late King James at the watter of Boyne'.[127] The earl of Leven, captain and governor of Edinburgh Castle, was ordered to fire the guns of Edinburgh Castle. Lord Cardross was to immediately write to the governors of Stirling and Dumbarton Castles respectively for their guns to be fired in celebration. Sir John Hall, provost of Edinburgh, was ordered to ensure that the bells within the city were rung and bonfires were ordered to be held so that 'all their Majesties good subjects may evidence and shew their joy and satisfactione for

---

122 Ibid., p. 316. 123 *Account of the proceedings of the estates*, vol. 1, p. 207. 124 Ibid.; McBride, *The siege of Derry*, pp 27–8. 125 *APS*, IX, 170. 126 Ibid. 127 *RPCS*, Third Series, vol. 15, p. 311.

so glorious a victorie'.[128] Such symbolism of so important a victory is particularly striking given the relatively recent experience of the bombardment of the
1689 convention from Edinburgh Castle by the Jacobite duke of Gordon. A
Proclamation for a Solemn and Public Thanksgiving was subsequently issued
by the Scottish privy council on behalf of William and Mary on 26 July 1690
to celebrate 'our glorious expeditione into, and the success of our armes within
our said kingdome of Ireland'.[129] The proclamation was ordered to be read out
from the pulpit 'in every paroch church and meeting house'.[130] This was to be
mandatory and failure to comply would result in punishment. Ministers were
to

> exhort all our subjects to a serious and devout performance of the saids
> prayers, praises and thanksgiveing as they tender the favor of the
> Almighty God, the preservatione of the Protestant religione and the
> safity and preservatione of our royall persone and government.[131]

Similar arrangements were made following news of the safe return of King
William from Waterford to England on 6 September 1690. On 11 September
the privy council ordered the bells to be rung in Edinburgh, bonfires were to
be held, and the guns of Edinburgh Castle were to be fired in celebration.[132] A
further proclamation was issued by the privy council on 17 September for a
Solemn and Public Thanksgiving to celebrate William's triumph in Ireland.
This was to be observed in the city of Edinburgh and the shires of Edinburgh,
Haddington and Linlithgow on Sunday 20 September. The remainder of the
country was to observe the Thanksgiving on Sunday 5 October.[133] The privy
council then wrote to William on 18 September congratulating William on his
triumph in Ireland:

> Wee cannot suficiently express our exceeding great joy for your
> Majesties safe returne and glorious success in your late expedition into
> Ireland. Your heroick couradge in exposing your sacred persone so fre-
> quently for the interest of religion and releiff of your subjects will tend
> to your immortall renoun and gives us present occassione to bless God
> for your preservatione.[134]

From an ecclesiastical perspective, the triumph of Presbyterianism in Scotland was fundamental to the wider struggle of international Protestantism, a
struggle which included the Irish situation. The ideology and mentality of this

128 Ibid.   129 Ibid., p. 335. The Solemn Thanksgiving was to be observed in all churches and
meeting houses south of the river Tay on Tuesday 5 August, whilst in the rest of the kingdom it
was to be observed on Tuesday 12 August.   130 Ibid.   131 Ibid.   132 Ibid., p. 429.   133 Ibid.,
p. 443.   134 Ibid., pp 443-4.

struggle, as perceived by the Scottish Presbyterian establishment, was encapsulated in the Act anent a Solemn National Fast and Humiliation, with the Causes thereof, of 12 November 1690. This was an act of the 1690 general assembly, the first general assembly to be held in Scotland since 1653. The main focus of the justification for a fast and humiliation lay with the need of moral purifcation and reformation with the extermination of sin from the land. Thus,

> Although our gracious God hath of late, for his own name sake, wrought great and wonderful things for Britain and Ireland, and for this Church and nation in particular, yet the inhabitants thereof have cause to remember their own evil ways, and to loathe themselves in their own sight for their iniquities.[135]

In addition, the act referred to the contemporary situation in the three kingdoms. Prayer was required to ensure that 'the Lord would preserve and bless our gracious King and Queen, William and Mary, and establish their throne by righteousness and religion, and grant to these nations peace and truth together'.[136] The safety, defence and promotion of international Calvinism was likewise emphasised. Firstly, it was emphasised that the Lord 'would pity his oppressed people the French Protestants, and gather them out of all the places whither they have been scattered in the cloudy and dark day'.[137] This was a clear reference to the persecution of the French Huguenots under Louis XIV following the revocation of the edict of Nantes in 1685, which resulted in the mass exodus of circa 250,000 French Protestants from France. This marked a long-term decline in the size of the French Protestant community. During the reign of Henry IV (1553-1610), the French Protestant population amounted to *circa* one million people. By 1660 this figure had declined to 765,000 and to 735,000 by 1680.[138] The Huguenot diaspora post-1685 extended to the Protestant safehavens of the United Provinces of the Dutch Republic, Brandenburg-Prussia, Scandinavia, Switzerland and North America. Some 10,000 refugees fled to Ireland with a further 40,000-50,000 relocating in England.[139] A Huguenot community was in existence in Edinburgh with its own minister, the Revd Mr. Dupont, and congregation.[140] In addition, two of

135 T. Pitcairn (ed.), *Acts of the general assembly of the Church of Scotland, 1638-1842* (Edinburgh, 1843), p. 228.   136 Ibid., p. 230.   137 Ibid.   138 J.B. Collins, *The state in early modern France* (Cambridge, 1995), p. 103.   139 See W.C. Scoville, *The persecution of Huguenots and French economic development, 1680-1720* (London, 1960), pp 98-130; T. Munck, *Seventeenth century Europe. State, conflict and the social order in Europe, 1598-1700* (London, 1990), pp 368-9.   140 R.D. Gwynn, *Huguenot heritage. The history and contribution of the Huguenots in Britain* (London, 1985), p. 38; S. Smiles, *The Huguenots. Their settlements, churches, & industries, in England and Ireland* (London, 1867), p. 338.

the 31 elders of the Threadneedle church of the French Church of London in the period 1698-1700 had been born in Pittenweem, Fife.[141] The transferable skills of the Huguenots were employed in the manufacture of papermaking in Scotland and England from the 1670s to the 1720s, whilst one Paul Romieu, a watchmaker and elder of the Edinburgh French Church, was admitted as a burgess of Edinburgh in 1676 due to the lack of watchmakers in the capital.[142] A colony of weavers from Picardy was involved in the manufacture of linen near the head of Leith Walk, whilst other Huguenot refugees opened a silk-factory.[143] The paternalistic outlook of the general assembly of the Church of Scotland as per 12 November 1690 must therefore be viewed in tandem with the raising of voluntary contributions. The Act anent a Solemn National Fast and Humiliation also expressed the hope that the Lord 'would be the defence, strength, and salvation of any of his people who are in war or danger, by infidel or Popish adversaries in Europe or America'.[144] In addition, the Irish situation was subject to special consideration:

> in particular, that the Lord would be gracious to Ireland, and sanctify to his people there both their distress and deliverance, and perfect what concerneth them; that he would *convert the natives there to the truth*, reduce that land to peace, and appoint salvation for walls and bulwarks to Britain.[145]

This language harks back to the three kingdom ideology of the Scottish Covenanting Movement, especially the Solemn League and Covenant of 1643 which sought to impose Presbyterianism in England and Ireland as well as in Scotland. Therefore, Ireland was not merely the military theatre of war in which James VII and II had been defeated by the forces of William of Orange. It also represented a geographical arena in which the forces of international Protestantism must triumph over the unconverted.

Despite the triumph of William at the Boyne and the treaty of Limerick of 1691 which ended the war in Ireland, the external threat of an Irish invasion and the internal threat of a further Jacobite rising remained real to the newly established regime in Scotland . On 11 May 1692 the royal burgh of Stirling, a key strategic location in the heart of Scotland *vis-à-vis* the threat of Highland Jacobitism, noted the prospect of a 'Designed invasion of French and Irish papists' and prepared to defend itself against such a threat.[146] As evidenced by the massacre of Glencoe in 1692, and the Jacobite risings of the eighteenth

---

141 Gwynn, *Huguenot heritage*, p. 153. 142 Ibid., pp 72-6. 143 Smiles, *The Huguenots*, p. 338. 144 *Acts of the general assembly of the Church of Scotland*, p. 230. 145 Ibid. These are my own italics. 146 R. Renwick (ed.), *Extracts from the records of the royal burgh of Stirling A.D. 1667-1752* (Glasgow, 1889), pp 66-7.

century, especially those of 1715 and 1745, Jacobitism posed a perennial threat to the strategic security of the military-fiscal British state.[147]

CONCLUSION

The Scottish response to the siege of Londonderry can be viewed from various perspectives and in a variety of contexts. The fact that Ulster had become a Scottish colony was reflected in the close cultural and ethnic links which had developed over the North Channel and the number of refugees who fled to Scotland when the troubles in Ireland broke out. Many of these refugees had originally migrated from Scotland, especially south-west Scotland, or were descended from Scottish migrant families. Irish Protestants were also particularly adept and proactive in petitioning Scottish national institutions for aid. The official Scottish response in terms of Church and State to the fate and condition of Irish and French Protestants was a sympathetic one, personified in voluntary contributions to ease their turmoil and improve their condition. In terms of military and strategic security of the Williamite regime in Scotland, the siege of Londonderry was not viewed as an isolated incident but as an integral component of the military clash between James VII and II and William of Orange. The external threat of a military invasion from Ireland was to be avoided at all costs, whilst the internal threat of Jacobitism (both politically and militarily) was to be neutralised. Ultimately, contemporary perceptions of the siege were embroiled not only with perceptions of the wider struggle of the war in Ireland, but also of arbitrary power and despotism. 'Popery' was equated with 'slavery', whilst the 'true reformed religion' was equated with 'liberty'.[148] Such a leitmotif became a dominant feature of the symbolism and language of the new Presbyterian regime in Scotland. Hence, it was argued that the crux of the struggle was not between William and James, nor between 'Protestant and Papist, but whether Great Britain and Ireland shall be preserved in their Religion, Laws, and Liberties, as they are; or whether they shall be conquered and subjected to French Tyranny, and Irish bloody Cruelty'.[149] Thus, the Protestants of Londonderry were described as 'brave'[150] and 'magnanimous'[151] and Williamite victory at the Boyne was recognised by state-sponsored celebrations in Scotland. Clear cultural and ethnic links were apparent in the contemporary Scottish response in 1689-90; links which were personified in symbolic language, celebration and triumphialism. Somewhat ironically, the two way process of links across the

---

147 G. Holmes & D. Szechi, *The age of oligarchy. Pre-industrial Britain 1722-1783* (London, 1993), pp 71-2, see also pp 89-100; Holmes, *The making of a great power*, pp 253-4. 148 *Account of the proceedings of the estates*, vol. 1, 111-2. See also, Ibid., pp 151-2. 149 *Account of the proceedings of the estates*, p. 100. 150 Ibid., p. 122. 151 Ibid., p. 111.

North Channel led to substantial Irish immigration, both Protestant and Catholic, into Scotland in the nineteenth century. The celebrations of fundamental icons in Protestant Ulster identity, notably the battle of the Boyne and the siege of Londonderry, thereby took on a new meaning for many Protestant migrants, the implications of which still hold importance for the future of modern Scottish society.[152]

152 See, for example, G. Walker & T. Gallagher (eds), *Sermons and battle hymns: Protestant popular culture in modern Scotland* (1990); T. Gallagher, *Glasgow: The uneasy peace* (1987).

The strange enigma of Oliver Goldsmith

Robert Welch

He may have 'written like an angel' but he also wrote like a machine. Goldsmith began his writing career in the middle of the eighteenth century, in a London which, through the development of newspapers, journals, annual registers, encyclopaedias, had become a kind of industrialised literary centre. While he was working as an assistant master at a school in Peckham on the outskirts of London in 1757 he met Ralph Griffiths, who took him on as an author for his *Monthly Review*. At this time he would write for five hours a day, so the link with industrialization is not inappropriate. In the following year, in 1758, he applied for a post as a surgeon in the East India Company, but failed to qualify, perhaps because of the ambiguity surrounding his medical qualifications: he studied at Trinity, Edinburgh, and Leiden (and possibly Louvain), but it is not certain that he ever took a medical degree. Failing to secure the job with the East India, then one of the biggest trading companies in the world, he resolved to set himself up as an author, a lowly trade, but one which could, given good fortune, good contacts, stamina, and some ability, lead to success and, hopefully, a decent living.

He is, in his choice of writing as a kind of business, an example of a new kind of author. Like Samuel Johnson, who became his friend, like Richard Steele, and like John O'Keefe, other Irishmen, he threw himself into the busy uncertainty of a life in London where he attempted to sustain himself through his literary efforts. These writers have this much in common: that they entered the market place of literature with no other support than that which they could supply from their own energy and imaginative invention. They were, at bottom, hacks. Patronage was over, apart from a few lucky souls who won the attention of a wealthy man: one of these lucky ones, was Mark Akenside, whose *Pleasures of Imagination* (1744) had considerable success. He enjoyed the support of Jeremiah Dyson, whom he had met while a student at Leiden. Or there was the fortunate Thomas Gray, whose fellowship at Pembroke College in Cambridge gave him the time and freedom to indulge his various enthusiasms for Celtic and Icelandic mythology, and to evoke a sweetly melancholic world-weariness in the *Elegy written in a County Churchyard* (1757).

Contrast for a moment Gray in the calm chambers of Pembroke, where the Fellows invited the Welsh harper 'Blind' Parry to play for them in 1757, to

Goldsmith at around this time, working for Griffiths, and one can gain some insight into the harshness of the marketplace of literary London for a writer with no support, inherited wealth, or patronage.

After he met his employer Goldsmith lived over Griffiths' book shop in Paternoster Row for five months, writing for his keep, and a small amount of money besides, his work being overseen daily by his landlord and his wife. Mr or Mrs Griffiths must have grown tired of their lodger because he was shortly on the move. He settled in various locations, one of them off Farfingdon Street near the Old Bailey, at the top of a flight of steps, known as Break Neck Steps. The locale was visited many years later by Washington Irving, who described the squalor, filth, and dinginess of the place: it was difficult to get to because of the lines of washing hung up every where along the back streets which were a huge collective laundry. A letter home to his friend at Trinity, Bob Bryanton describes his situation in February 1759. He is aged 31 but already, he says, poverty and hardship have taken their toll:

> Imagine to yourself a pale melancholy visage, With two great wrinkles between the eyebrows, with an eye disgustingly severe, and a big wig . . . I can neither laugh nor drink; have contracted a hesitating, disagreeable manner of speaking, and a visage that looks ill-nature itself, in short I have thought myself into a settled melancholy, and an utter disgust of all that life brings with it.

Whatever about the 'disagreeable' way he spoke (Garrick's joke that he talked like poor poll comes to mind, as does Burke's recollection that he never lost the Irish brogue) nevertheless his writing skills were such that he began to be much in demand. Even at this stage he was capable of writing tersely and in an informed and vivid way about a whole variety of subjects: essays; sketches; meditations; reflections on taste; biography – he wrote a *Life of Voltaire* whom he had met in Lausanne; and reflections on learning, manners, and cultural differences. As Seamus Deane has said, he was a writer who felt himself part of a European culture of rational enlightenment, which still retained the idea that it was possible for a civilized intelligence to take the entire domain of human knowledge as its sphere. And as a writer of the enlightenment he would feel it part of his duty to disseminate understanding by discerning in the variety of human experience common laws and persuasions. No one now pretends to anything like this 'extensive view' in Samuel Johnson's phrase, but Goldsmith's willingness to use his expository and analytical talents across the whole range of natural and human history was not just a means of earning his bread. His tireless descriptions and evaluations, of subjects ranging from biology to English, Roman, and Greek history; the manners of the fashionable set at Bath to the role of universities in European culture; the place of emotion in society to the forms of government suitable for different peoples; – all of these indicate an industry driven by an ideal of culture and writing as a thing to be shared in common in a civilized community. His was a syncretic and evaluative mind; his style, famously lucid and natural, was one which sought to engage the reader's interest while stimulating him (or her) to a broader and more enlightened conception.

He loves describing scenes of shared understanding, of mutuality. He is a writer of *communitas* who celebrates the experience of belonging together in society, where the individual is valued and appreciated as a part, however small, in the great apparatus of integrated life that social reality should, ideally, be. And to be the kind of author Goldsmith wished to be, was to be responsible for maintaining a clear view of the interconnectedness of all human interests; hence Goldsmith's apparently foolhardy venturings into a bewildering array of widely-disparate fields.

It wasn't simply necessity that drove him to such variety; nor was it the vanity of intellect that allows itself an opinion on anything under the sun; it was the responsible exercise of an integrating intelligence. His ability in this regard naturally commanded him to editors: he wrote for Tobias Smollett's *Critical Review*, and for John Newbery's *Public Ledger*, contributing the *Citizen of the World* to the latter between 1760 and 1761.

The gap between the ideal universal intelligence of the enlightened man and the harshness of actuality is evident in circumstances in which he wrote *The Citizen of the World*. As with Griffiths he was a lodger; this time, however, in better accommodation, in Wine Office Court, Fleet Street, his landlord being a relative of his new employer, Newbury. Goldsmith seems to have entrusted Newbury with his financial affairs, because when he moved to another house in Islington, owned by an Elizabeth Fleming, Newbury undertook to pay his rent and deduct this amount from what was due to him for his writings. However, relations between them seem to have come to a sorry pass, because in 1764 Samuel Johnson received a distressed note from his friend in Islington, telling him that the landlady Mrs Fleming, had had him detained under house arrest for debt – the same situation the good-natured Honeywood finds himself in in *The Good-Natur'd Man* (1768). Johnson, so we are told in *Boswell's Life*, immediately sent him a guinea,

> And promised to come to him directly. I accordingly went as soon as I was dressed . . . I perceived that he had already changed my guinea, and had got a bottle of Madeira and a glass before him. I put the cork into the bottle, desired he should be calm, and began to talk to him of the means by which he might be extricated. He then told me he had a novel ready for the press, which he then produced to me. I looked into it, and saw its merit; told the landlady, I should soon return; and, having gone to a bookseller, sold it for £60.

This was *The Vicar of Wakefield*, published in 1766. It is a study of the problems encountered by the enlightened man, motivated by principles of universal benevolence and the spirit of *communitas*, in a world driven by power, money, and lust. It is, without a shadow of doubt, based on Goldsmith's own experiences of growing up in an Irish family, where kindness and decency towards others were the governing principles. In Letter 22 of *The Citizen of the World*, which gives the history of the Man in Black – another autobiographical figure – Goldsmith tells how this personage has grown careful in a world which exploits readily those qualities of universal benevolence inculcated into his children by the father of the Man in Black:

> We were taught to consider all the interests of mankind as our own; to regard the human face divine with affection and esteem; he worked us up to be mere machines of pity, and rendered us incapable of withstanding the slightest impulse made either by real or fictitious distress. I resembled, upon my first entrance into the busy and insidious world, one of those gladiators, who were exposed without armour in the amphitheatre at Rome.

The *Vicar of Wakefield* paints a deeply moving picture of a good man surrounded by a loving family. A 'prose-idyll', Goethe called it, and its evocation of kindness beset by perfidy deeply affected him as young man. Goldsmith calls into our imaginations a scene, setting and people with which we are all familiar: it is the good place, the scene of happy content, joyous company, easy and natural relationships. Nature and man are at peace with each other, and the community is bound together in a mutuality that accepts gradations of skill and ability effortlessly because all are equally valued. It is a free and open human space. The house the Primroses live in has one story; it is thatched which gives it 'an air of snugness'; the walls inside are 'nicely' whitewashed; outside there are 'little enclosures' of elm and hedge which have an inexpressible beauty'. This is a 'little republic' (a bit like Tom Paulin's dream of a 'sweet equal republic') regulated by the gentle and uncoercive laws established by Dr Primrose himself, whose whole moral and intellectual being is concentrated upon two concerns: sympathy for others, and truth. This is the 'human face divine' of *The Citizen of the World*; it is the face of Goldsmith's own beloved father; and it is the face of Christ. However, as he recounts in his Life of Voltaire, when the young Voltaire had spent days in his room trying to devise an equable system for social behaviour, his father brought him into his own room and, showing him the crucifix, declared; 'behold the fate of reformers'.

And indeed Dr Primrose is to be mutilated and crucified, spiritually, morally, and even physically. The still peace of Goethe's prose idyll is invaded by the insatiable drives of Squire Thornhill's lust and malignancy, but before his real nature is revealed the Primrose family discover the instability of their own judgements in their confused and rash reactions to the carefully orchestrated enticements and the alluring but at the same time disturbing charade Thornhill arranges to delude Deborah, the Vicar's wife, and his two daughters, Sophia and Olivia. Two whores are engaged to masquerade as women of quality Lady Blarney (ominously titled) and Wilheimina Amelia Skeggs – and their mission is to induct the two girls into the attractions and excitements of the vice-business which he runs in the town. The whores are sufficiently blatant in their behaviour to send out warning signals, and Mr Burchell (who is to be the final benefactor who will resolve all in the end), a seemingly impoverished friend of the family, explicitly warns against the two prostitutes and their insolent and insouciant pimp. However, Deborah is hooked by the allure of advantageous contacts in town. The Vicar tries to remain neutral but eventually Mr Burchell is banished from Dr Primrose's now well-breached citadel of integrity and peace. The instability of moral truth in the varying circumstance of life is brilliantly conveyed in the manner in which the Vicar himself stifles his own qualms of conscience at getting rid of such an obviously decent man as Mr Burchell. Indeed he is pleased to be rid of the inconvenience of being reminded of the depth of his own misgivings, and this leads to a harrowing generalization to conclude a chapter which reveals benevolence and truth to be in short supply when power and wealth combine to make us believe what we want to believe, even though there still remains a part of the mind (the conscience) which misgives:

> Conscience is a coward; and those faults it has not strength enough to prevent, it seldom has justice enough to accuse.

This quality of spare, intensely-experienced, weighty writing, is what drew the admiration of Johnson and Edward Burke.

This is no easy moral maxim: it is a hard-won insight wrung from the depths of experience. The citadel of truth is fissiparous with our own weaknesses which combine with what the traditional moral teachings used to call 'an inclination to evil' to make the citadel of peace and truth deeply unstable in the face of underground upheaval or direct attack. An image Goldsmith frequently turns to is the just town under siege from the forces of evil.

One of the ways in which Goldsmith's creative mind works, perhaps one of its most characteristic modes of procedure, is to translate particular incidents into general moral understandings. These general moral observations, arrived at through weighing the particulars, diversify into political and legal considerations, provoking Goldsmith's ethical sense into judicial concerns and issues of state. Here, I believe, he was deeply influential on his friend Edmund Burke, one of the great innovators in British constitutional thought; and if that is so, then Goldsmith too may be regarded as a very significant person in the development of modern British political philosophy.

Goldsmith has recourse to the image of the city under siege on a number of occasions. As an Irish Protestant, he would be deeply sensitive to the complex of powerful feelings and attitudes attached to the concept of siege: liberty, internal dishonesty, power, the need to combine against a seemingly irresistible aggressor, strength in adversity, honour, and so on. The walls of Derry. In a critical passage in *The Vicar of Wakefield* the concept of siege is reworked, and linked to freedom, the people, and loyalty to the crown. This network of ideas, revolving around a central preoccupation with the nature of British (including English and Irish) liberty, I feel, deeply influenced Burke's more comprehensive explorations of the relationship between freedom and order.

The Vicar's argument is engaged with someone whom he presumes to be the master of a house where he has been invited for the night, when in fact it is the butler pretending to be the landlord in his employees absence. In the course of the evening, this presumptuous servant declares himself to be against too extensive an exercise of royal power. The Vicar smells a republican, and enters into a long defence of the role of the monarchy in mitigating the powers of vested interests in a state, in particular by curtailing the arrogance of the rich, thereby protecting the people. The 'people', the generality of the middle order of people (which would, of course, exclude the poor, and the majority of Goldsmith's fellow-countrymen, whether in Ireland or in England), are protected by the king because he 'divides the power of the rich'; were he not to do this they, the rich, would fall on those beneath them, i.e. the middle order. These are like a town under siege by the wealthy, to which the king, the governor, is trying to bring in relief. While fear of the governors relief forces remains the rich offer blandishments to the besieged town, but once the threat of his assistance is removed the walls can easily be breached. Fear of might mitigates abuse. Fear of authority preserves freedom. Authority is necessary to protect liberty. Anyone, the Vicar argues, who pretends that liberty can subsist without authority is a liar. He then moves to the brilliant conclusion:

> I have known many of these pretended champions of liberty in my time, yet I do not remember one that was not in his heart and in his family a tyrant.

This addition of domestic circumstances to what would otherwise be abstract speculations on the nature of government is what Burke learned from Goldsmith; it brings the reasoning home by grounding it in ordinary experience, and it gives principle the force of personal emotion.

We see too, incidentally, that a different kind of Vicar emerges in these passages from the namby-pamby sentimental character he is sometimes assigned in commentary. His goodness and innocence is not stupidity: he can be (and is) taken advantage of, but his kindness has strength because it is allied to conviction, a conviction Goldsmith implies is grounded in the simplicity of truth. However, he cannot be left to his own devices; like mankind itself, he has to be saved and he is saved by a father figure, Sir William Thornhill, the hidden *deus ex machina* who has been their (spurned) friend Mr Burchell. Sir William (surely the name is deliberate?) comes, like the king, to the rescue of the Primroses who are all in jail through the devices of the evil nephew, the trafficker in vice, the pimp (who uses Catholic priests to ensnare young girls into whoredom) Squire Thornhill. William rescues the besieged. It is the keystone of Burke's thinking in *Reflections upon the Revolution in France* (1791) that the Glorious Revolution of 1688, which installed King William, was the means whereby the British constitution protected and maintained its ancient freedoms. Sir William, in Goldsmith's story, relieves the distress and misery of a British family caused when their innate naivete and goodness have been taken advantage of by the machinations of the vicious, who will use the simulacra of faith, in the form of bogus Catholic weddings, to compound their abominations. To be a 'machine of pity' is dangerous in a world containing those who know well how to trigger feeling for their own bad purposes.

Goldsmith's first comedy, *The Good Natur'd Man* (1768), which was rejected by Garrick for Drury Lane before being accepted at Covent Garden, translates the theme of the vulnerability of unprotected and impulsive goodness into the mixed and mobile environment of stage action. The dangers of feeling are explored, as in *The Vicar of Wakefield*, but private circumstances and concerns are linked to general themes of power and corruption. Goldsmith's friend, Johnson, was alive to the larger political implications of the play, and the vulnerability of creativity itself, when he wrote his prologue to the piece:

> The great 'tis true, can charm the electing tribe;
> The bard may supplicate, but cannot bribe.

How 'the great may operate is hinted at in the character of Lofty, someone who, though in reality a charlatan, passes himself off as a power-broker who has at his disposal all the necessary information for insider dealing and trafficking in offices. Lofty wishes to pass himself off as one of those who can put his supplicants into places through bribery, a nod, and a wink. He is one of those from whom the people need to be protected, as the king protects the town under siege in the *Vicars* political allegory. Here is Lofty on how he does business. He has already claimed that it was he who secured Sir William Honeywood his place. (Again William, and again here it is Sir William who is going to untie the knot that will release his nephew from the bind he has bed himself in through his 'good nature'.) Miss Richland, pretending to be amazed at Lofty's influence, gushes 'you courtiers can do anything, I see', to which Lofty replies:

> My dear madam, all this is but a mere exchange; we do greater things for one another everyday. Why, as thus, now: let me suppose you the First Lord of the Treasury, you have an employment in you that I want and I have a place in me that you want: do we here, do you there: interest of both side, few words, flat, done and done, and its over.

The cant of the knowing man; the effrontery of the insider letting you know *he* is on the inside and you're not; the assurance of the powerful: – all these are conveyed and mocked at in this bditiant speech. The likes of Lofty are given their power by the rich who hold the people under siege, who affront freedom and truth. The countervailing force must be true authority, vested in the king in the Vicar's philosophy; here in Sir William Honeywood himself who unmasks the hypocrisy of Lofty and also who reveals to this nephew the dangers of too reckless a sympathy. 'Our bounty', says Sir William, commenting on his nephew who has ruined himself through his benevolence, 'like a drop of water, disappears when diffused too widely'. Young Honeywood's sympathies are so promiscuously exercised that he actually cannot make up his mind one way or another about how one should deal with anything, even a threat of being blown up. Mr and Mrs Croaker receive such a threat: she believes that the way to deal with this kind of thing is to ignore it, or to pay the extortionists what they want and have done with it; he, on the other hand, claims that the best course of action is to downface them. Honeywood, whose opinion they solicit, veers first one way, then the other, to which Mrs Croaker responds that she and her husband both can't be right. In exasperation she exclaims: 'My hat must be on my head, or my hat must be off.'

The terrible susceptability of good nature to impressions can, as this play shows, lead to a quaking uncertainty, and unless protected, to personal and financial ruin. *She Stoops to Conquer* (1773) performed the year before Goldsmith died, is his most achieved and assured work, apart from *The Deserted Village* (1770). *She Stoops to Conquer*, contrary to what has sometimes been slackly asserted, that the play has little or no depth, is a profoundly realized depiction of moral, personal, and economic uncertainty. It is sub-titled 'The Mistakes of a Night, and the play is a kind of nocturnal adventure into a world where all certainty is lost, where people do not know who and what they are; they are ignorant of those to whom they speak; they assume false assurance; they buy illusion and they think they can have everything they want at a price. This isn't the English or the Irish countryside: is a territory of the mind, visited by Shakespeare in *A Midsummer Nights Dream*, that sombre comedy of sexual and political trouble; and by Beckett in all of his plays and novels. Its a place where everything is contingent. The theme of the vulnerability of good-ness is left behind to face the larger metaphysic of profound not-knowing.

Not only can Marlow, the peculiar hero of this play, not talk with women of any reputation, he cannot even look at them; but he is an overweening boor with women whom he regards as his inferiors. This has something to do with class but it has more to do with what Marlows much more normal friend Hastings calls 'assurance'. Marlow has no settled personal identity; he has no core of reality; no fixed sense of the truth of what he is. Terrifyingly and comically this comes out in his conversations with Kate Hardcastle. In the first instance when she is herself, he cannot bring himself to raise his eyes to her, and she has to complete all his attempts at terse and worldly-wise observations. Here she is completing a lame observation on hypocrisy he has been trying to formulate:

> You mean that in this hypocritical age there are few that do not con-demn in public what they practice in private, and think they pay every debt to virtue when they praise it.

Compare the halting and embarrassed set of exchanges of which this forms part, to the brilliant and dashing dialogue between the two when he believes she's a serving maid. Goldsmith's focus is on the exercise of raw sexual power, driven by the assurance a consciousness of superiority brings. Power, and not just sexual power, will extend its prerogative as far as it can unless checked by true authority, integrity, and honesty. Here again he is a moralist; and despite all the roistering fun of the play (Tony Lumpkin in the ale house, the trick Tony plays on Marlow, the ludicrous and hectic drive through the night end-ing up in the muddy pond back where they started), despite all the brio, there is a gloomy side to it emanating from the sense of there being nothing to Marlow other than a string of opportunistic and exploitative impulses. He is, in a very real sense, a much greater lout than poor Tony Lumpkin, and it is to point this up that Lumpkin has his morally-structured place in the dramatic action.

Goldsmith conveys a deeply disquieting sense that, for all the effort of the enlightenment, to the English phase of which he contributed in no small way himself, there remains something dark and irredeemable in human nature and in human affairs. He dreamed of rest and purity, and his *Deserted Village* embodies a lost ideal of peace, safety, and love. But it is gone. And what is left to Goldsmith? The role of an author. In his *Inquiry into the Present State of Polite Learning* (1759) one of his first sustained pieces of writing, he had writ-ten of the author that he was 'a thing only to be laughed at. His person, not his jest, becomes the mirth of the company. At his approach the most fat unthink-ing face brightens into malicious meaning.'

To be an author was to be the butt of jokes, the object of disregard at best, contempt and disdain at worst. The lost ideal of a place to be at home has gone; 'the lovely bowers of innocence and ease' have been rudely forced. Authorship and authority are a joke; misprisions abound; there is no stability, no assurance in human transaction. To be brought up to be 'a machine of pity' unfits one for survival in a world where all is power. At the end of *The Deserted Village* all are leaving for another shore:

> Downward they move, a melancholy band,
> Pass from the shore, and darken all the strand.

And what of poetry, what of that art which above all others drew him? He describes poetry as

> My shame in crowds, my solitary pride . . .

She is 'the guide by which the nobler arts excel'; she is the 'nurse of virtue'. But he even bids her farewell. In a final and confused act of benevolence to humanity he prays that she, poetry, may continue to impart the wisdom to human kind that only she can:

> Teach every man to spurn the rage of gain:
> Teach him that states of native strength possest,
> Through very poor, may still be very blest;
> That trade's proud empire hastes to swift decay,
> As ocean sweeps the laboured mole away;
> While self-dependent power can time defy,
> As rocks resist the billows and the sky.

Poetry may teach one to be as impervious as rock to the billows and the turbulent sky. It may develop a 'self-dependent powee and improve the 'states of native strength'. But will it? This is a heart-smitten wish by a gloomy and tormented man, whose kindness and humanity have got him nowhere.

Three drunken nights and a hangover: the siege, the Apprentice Boys and Irish national identity, 1779-80

Breandan Mac Suibhne

In the late eighteenth century Derry was the hub of a region that extended from the Sperrins in the east, south to Bearnasomre and west to the Rosses. Within this region, a fertile district between Letterkenny, Limavady and Strabane formed an advantaged core zone, the inhabitants of which were pre-dominantly Protestant with Presbysterians outnumbering Episcopalians in all localities. Critically, a profound tension had characterised the whole commu-nity in this area since the early 1700s. Notwithstanding the centrality of the siege of Derry in the 'Glorious Revolution', William King (1650-1729), the bishop of Derry (1690-1703), became a vocal proponent of the penal laws that ejected Presbyterians from the polity. Presbyterian resentment went beyond opposition to rectors and tithes to a more general antipathy to Episcopalians. 'Scotch' verse – a self-conscious amplification of social and cultural difference – was a conspicuous feature of regional print culture from the 1730s. Faction-fighting between the 'Scotch laddies' of Strabane, a Presbyterian town, and the 'English' of Lifford, its Episcopalian suburb, continued until the late 1700s. A levelling republican sub-culture developed that included a cult of Oliver Cromwell; Presbyterian radicals drank to the memory of the Protector and named their sons after him. From mid-century, this tension deepened as Presbyterians made considerable social advances on the back of the region's buoyant flax-centred economy without enjoying significant political gains. As the Protestant bloc fractured – and as the emergence of an English-speaking Catholic middle-class fractured 'the other' – simple oppositions of Planter – artisans and tradesmen, merchants, ministers and manufacturers, farmers and smallholders – conceived their ideological project as drawing a 'veil of obliv-ion' over divisive settler and native narratives of the Irish past and uniting people of diverse religious and cultural backgrounds in order to pursue their common 'national' interest. In the 1780s they gave this project practical expression: they enrolled (and armed Catholics) in volunteer companies; paraded at the Catholic bishop's house in Derry to celebrate their political vic-tories; supported the extension of the franchise to propertied Catholics; raised money for the erection of chapels (sixteen in the diocese of Raphoe 'in the space of a few years' and a considerable number in the Derry diocese including the city's Long Tower Church) and in some instances attended the first mass in these chapels when they opened.[1]

The commemoration of the siege of Derry has long been associated with sectarian coat-trailing and, more recently, assertions of an ambiguous loyalty to the British crown; in recent years in particular, unionists have used the commemoration to sustain the myth of a monolithic anything-but-Irish Protestant community locked into conflict with an equally homogenous 'mere Irish' Catholic community that can never be trusted. The experience of late eighteenth century Derry, however, cannot be shoe-horned into this dreary steeples view of Irish history.

The deep social, cultural and political divisions that separated Presbyterians and Episcopalians rendered notions of a monolithic Protestant community redundant: there was no 'faithful tribe'. Nor were all Catholics raking the ashes of seventeenth century losses: many Micks and Marys were unapologetically on the make, abandoning the Irish language, Charlie-over-the waterism and wilder superstitions of their country cousins as they clambered up the social ladder. Furthermore, sectarian exclusion was increasingly a thing of the past: again, Protestants were falling over themselves to build chapels for Catholics in the 1780s; Catholic clergy and laymen had little difficulty in accepting the herectics' money (or giving them money to purchase arms) and the disappearance of 'He must be a Protestant' from job advertisements in the press indicated voluntary movement towards fair employment practices.

This chapter illuminates the political malleability of the commemoration of the siege by recalling three drunken nights in Derry during this period of ideological and political change. The first drunken night establishes that Irish national identity was constructed in opposition to a British 'other'; the second illustrates that this identity was inclusive, embracing Catholic, Protestant and Dissenter, and the third elaborates the version of Irish history that was to enable people of such diverse religious and cultural backgrounds to overlook past sufferings and enjoy a future of freedom, prosperity and happiness. On the second and third occasions, the proponents of this new dispensation in Irish society dramatically commemorated the siege.

---

1 B. Mac Suibhne, 'Patriot Paddies: the Volunteers and Irish identity in northwest Ulster, 1778-86' (unpublished PhD dissertation Carnegie Mellon University, 1998).

THE FIRST DRUNKEN NIGHT

The first drunken night occurred on Tuesday 30 November 1779. Dublin newspapers received in Derry the previous evening had brought confirmation that the House of Commons on College Green had refused to vote for new taxes unless the British cabinet relaxed its restraints on Irish trade. This massive victory for the Patriot party owed much to the threat of violence from Volunteer companies. These companies were local paramilitary associations formed throughout Ireland from spring 1778 to defend their communities in the event of a French landing when regular British troops were fighting 'rebels' in America. Initially, they confined their activities to military training yet in spring 1779 when the economic 'distress' caused by Britain's war in America became widely felt they threw their weight behind a 'buy Irish' campaign; the public were urged to choose Irish goods in preference to British products in order to assist distressed Irish manufacturers. When parliament reconvened in October Volunteers pressed members to pass a 'short money bill' – allocation of revenue for a six month as opposed to a two year period – unless the British cabinet made substantial concessions.

By early November, there had been a real sense that violence would erupt if parliament did not vote 'for the good of Ireland, for a free trade, and a short money bill'. Dublin Volunteers parading on College Green had trained a field-piece on parliament house; a sign hanging on the gun read 'A Free Trade or This'. In the northwest, growing militancy had been evident in sermons delivered to Volunteer companies by Presbyterian ministers: in September the Revd William Crawford had preached to the Strabane Rangers on 'the connection betwixt courage and moral virtue'; in October the Strabane Rangers and the Strabane, Fin-Water and Urney Volunteers had heard the Revd Andrew Alexander reflect on 'the advantages of a general knowledge of the use of arms' and at the height of the crisis in mid-November the Revd Hugh Delap had explained to the Omagh and Cappagh Volunteers that magistrates and politicians were not appointed by the Almighty and that were times when citizens were justified in opposing them.[2] In contrast, yet also reflecting fears that a violent clash was imminent, the Catholic clergy in the diocese of Derry had read an address in all their places of worship on Sunday 7 November reminding their congregations of the 'fidelity and obedience justly due to our most gracious Sovereign King George the Third and all those constituted in dignity over us'; the priests urged 'humble submission to all those in power' and

2 W. Crawford, *The connection betwixt courage and the moral virtues* (Strabane, 1779); A. Alexander, *The advantages of a general knowledge of the use of arms* (Strabane, 1779); H. Delap, *An inquiry, whether, and how far, magistracy if of a divine appointment, and of the subjection due thereunto* (Strabane, 1779).

warned their congregations' against the illusions and idle suggestions of designing enemies who, by engaging you in any measures contrary to the interest of the present government, would only lead you to your ruin, by making you the instruments of their policy, rather than the objects of their care'; they should behave as 'good Christians and faithful subjects' during 'this interesting emergency'.[3]

In this context, 'general joy' greeted the news that parliament had voted 'for the good of Ireland'; there was satisfaction that parliament was demanding that restraints on Ireland's commercial freedom be loosened yet also relief that violence had been avoided. George Douglas, the editor of the London-Derry *Journal*, was ecstatic. Putting his paper to bed on Tuesday morning, he dropped several advertisements to make space for the parliamentary debates and, in place of the usual local items, he simply instructed the 'friends to the Freedom and Prosperity of 'IRELAND' to assemble at the town hall at seven o'clock that evening with bottles of 'IRISH liquor' to drink success to 'the ever glorious Majority in OUR House of Commons, who, like true Patriots, and HONEST Irishmen, refused to vote for "New Taxes without a FREE TRADE".[4] The drinking Derryman had not been born who would have had to be told twice; styling themselves 'true-born patriot Paddies', the 'friends of Ireland and Freedom' assembled at the town hall and drank 'whiskey in every possible modification, currant, raspberry, mixed, plain, &c. &c.' to celebrate Ireland's prosperity, freedom and constitutional independence; according to a report in the *Journal*, 'some drank out of Irish naggins, whilst others had the feet of their glasses broken off, and the want supplied by potatoes'.[5]

The meaning of 'Paddies' drinking 'Irish liquor' from glasses propped up by potatoes is unequivocal. Paddy, whiskey and potatoes were central to negative British stereotypes of Irish people: Paddy was the dumb archetypal Irishman; whiskey was the 'Irish disease' – it made Paddy lazy, irrational and violent – and the potato was a lazy crop grown by lazy people in lazy beds. The drunken Derrymen staggering around the town hall were quite clear-headed about their identity: no matter how disdained on the neighbouring island, they were Irish.

THE SECOND DRUNKEN NIGHT

But who were the Paddies? One can assume that most of those who assembled in the town hall were Protestants, mainly Presbyterians; was this, then, the rise of a 'Protestant nation' or did this nation include Catholics? The 'True-born Patriot Paddies' were on the rip again a week later and this second drunken

3 *London-Derry Journal*, 16 Nov. 1779.   4 Ibid., 30 Nov. 1779.   5 Ibid., 3 Dec. 1779.

night provided an answer. The seventh of December was the anniversary of the shutting of the gates in 1688; although there had been sporadic commemorations of the relief (1 August 1689), there was no 'tradition' of commemorating the siege.[6] On 7 December 1779, however, the four city Volunteer companies paraded at noon, fired three volleys and then 'went through the ceremony of shutting the gates'; in doing so, they effectively inaugurated the (not unbroken) tradition of December commemorations. That evening the Apprentice Boys – A Volunteer company established by city tradesmen in 1778 which was the first organisation to adopt that name – 'entertained' their officers in the town hall which was illuminated and adorned with 'emblematical transparencies'.[7] In the course of the evening they sang a raucous song called 'Paddy's Triumph' to the tune 'Maggy Lowther'. This song concisely expresses the central conceit in modern Irish nationalism: Britain had divided the people of Ireland along religious lines in her own selfish interest; the people – Catholic, Protestant and Dissenter – must unite under the common name of Irishman (or Paddy); only then would Ireland have a harmonious relationship with her neighbour:[8]

> Come all you kind and loving souls,
> And join your own dear Paddy,
> With Irish liquor fill your bowls,
> And drink our friends that steady:
> Our Parliament of Paddies all,
> Of Irish manufacture.
> Who've laid the corner-stone of all,
> Our Irish architecture.
> And please the Lord, we'll raise it high,
> In spite of opposition,
> Tho'England storm, and Sawney cry,
> We'll hold our disposition,

6 J. Hempton, *Siege and history of Londonderry* (Dublin, 1861), p. 419 claims 7 December was first marked in 1775; although historians have repeated this claim, I am not aware of any contemporary reference to a December commemoration in 1775. 7 *L.J.*, 10 Dec. 1779; the report does not indicate that the Apprentice Boys performed the shutting of the gates but they would do so in subsequent years. Initially, the tradesmen had called their company the Mitchelburne Volunteers in commemoration of Col. John Mitchelburne, one of the joint governors of Derry during the siege; the Mitchelburne Club, a tradesmen's political association, had instigated the formation of the company. This name, however, was controversial as Presbyterians regarded Mitchelburne as the real hero of the siege not the more famous Revd George Walker who had downplayed Presbyterians' role in his *True account of the siege of London-Derry* (London, 1689). Following the election of William Lecky, a city merchant and former mayor, to the captaincy of the company, it adopted the more neutral name which was usually rendered as 'Prentice Boys'; see *L.J.*, 16 June, 3 July. 1778. 8 *L.J.*, 21 Dec. 1779.

Tho' Paddy has been mock'd to scorn,
For being poor and needy,
He has a soul can stand a storm,
From Britons rich and greedy.
Long, long, dear friends, we have been fools,
Divided in religion;
By this, to foes we have been tools,
And Paddy was their pigeon –
But Luther, Calvin, and the Pope
Now drink their jug of whiskey,
Shake hands, and join in one great hope,
And swear they'll get all tipsy!
Our Volunteers now fire their rounds,
There's FREEDOM in their thunder,
THEY first pour'd balm in Paddy's wounds,
And made our foes knock under!
THEY make our Court'ers Patriots,
Our Patriots more steady,
From Bourbon's league THEY sav'd our cots,
And Britons court bold Paddy!
But far it is from Paddy's mind,
To quarrel with his brethren:
To love and peace he is inclin'd,
With Britons first of all men.
One King, one Law – each country claim,
And EQUAL share of Freedom;
When Paddy's worth can that obtain,
He'll fight when Britons need him,
Then celebrate, my boys, this night,
The seventh of December,
When Volunteers of eighty-eight,
Were Derry's great defender.
The blood then young, now grown to age,
By feeding on its glory,
Will stem corruption's baneful rage,
And raise a prouder story.

THE THIRD DRUNKEN NIGHT

For Catholic Protestant and Dissenter to unite - as the Apprentice Boys proposed - they would have to dray a 'veil of oblivion' over divisive versions of the

past. Catholics would have to forget their woeful tales about dispossession by 'foreign' planters and, likewise, Protestants would have to obliterate the glorious myth of a band of settlers who had introduced civilisation into an alien environment yet had to remain watchful lest the natives skulk down from the mountains and massacre them as they had done in 1641. The third drunken night provided a clear elaboration of an alternative history of Ireland which, by downplaying the events of the seventeenth century, gave this multi-cultural Irish nation an historical anchor.

In winter 1779-80, Patriots had pocketed the concession of 'free trade' and turned their attention to legislative independence; specifically, they sought the repeal of Poynings' Law and the Declaratory Act (6 Geo. I, c. 5), the legislative double-lock that subordinated College Green to Westminster. In this campaign, they were eager to establish that Ireland not only had the right but also the capacity to be free; in other words, Ireland was in no way inferior to Britain and, as Alexander Montgomery of Convoy, Donegal's Independent MP, expressed it, Ireland's relationship to her neighbour should be that of a 'sister country' not a child to a 'selfish step-mother'.[9] Consequently, there was a concerted effort to develop local Volunteer companies into 'the Volunteer army of Ireland'. Companies united to form regiments or battalions and became sticklers for military protocol, asserting their equality with regulars on public occasions, insisting on silence in the ranks and neat uniforms, instituting courts martial to punish wayward members and even burying deceased members with military honours: incidentally, the first paramilitary funeral in the northwest took place on 10 December, three days after the first commemoration of the siege; the deceased, the Revd Thomas Torrens, had been chaplain of the Apprentice Boys and one can not help wondering if the first two drunken nights contributed to his demise.[10]

Armies, of course must be able to fight and at no stage since the formation of the first companies in 1778 had any Volunteers in the northwest proved themselves anything other than toy soldiers. However, in April 1780, Derry Patriots announced plans for a three day grand review to be held in the city in August; initially, it was intended that the review begin on 1 August, the anniversary of the relief, but this was subsequently changed to 9 August.[11] 'Over forty thousand' admiring spectators attended - an immense crowd before railway in a city of about 8,000 inhabitants - to watch 2,737 Volunteers participate in open-air war games. On the first day, companies and battalions arriving in the city drew up on the Diamond where they were assigned billets and then dismissed to enjoy the delights of the maiden city. On the second day, the battalions were divided into two brigades. Lord Charlemont reviewed the first brigade (Limavady, Strabane and Derry Battalions) while the second brigade

9 Ibid. 10 Ibid., 14 Dec. 1779. 11 Ibid., 21 Apr., 16 May. 1780.

(Glendermot, Raphoe, Tyrone and Donegal Battalions) held back the crowd. There was then a massive mock battle for the village of Upper Creggan; for several hours the two 'armies' advanced and retreated through the village firing powder until the first brigade finally withdrew. On the third day, Charlemont reviewed the second brigade. After the review, the first brigade took up defensive positions outside the city; when the second brigade attacked, they retreated through the gates which the Apprentice Boys closed behind; they then maintained 'heavy fire' from the walls before sallying out through Butcher Gate and Bishop Gate and routing the attackers.[13]

Most Volunteers were young men in their teens or early twenties and, needless to mention, there was a lot of drink taken over the three days; special consignments of 'Irish porter' were stockpiled for the occasion and in the weeks that followed companies inserted notices in the press thanking those who had 'entertained' them in the city.[13] No doubt, many of those who crowded into Derry's tap-rooms, taverns, inns and shebeens would have read or heard recited 'St Patrick's Address to the Irish Volunteers'. Composed by a city poet who signed himself 'O', it appeared on the front page of the *Journal* on the last day of the review. It describes how St Patrick had appeared to a sleeping Volunteer and related the history of Ireland. Critically, the patron overlooked both Catholic and Protestant sufferings in the seventeenth century and located the pivotal event in Irish history several hundred years earlier when Henry II had conspired with Dermot McMurrough to place Hibernia under 'a foreign sway': now, however, when the Volunteers' were reclaiming Ierne's (Erin's) freedom, the future was bright:[14]

> Deep sunk from reverie to rest,
> Gay visions dan'd before my eyes;
> No more by want or care oppress'd,
> Ideal bliss the scene supplies.
> Entranc'd in extacies I lay,
> When lo! A form before me stood,
> Whose smiles, benignant as the day,
> With rapture thrall'd my glowing blood.
> Refulgent rays his head surround,
> His beard descend'd on his breast,
> His flowing mantle swept the ground –
> Hibernia's Patron stood confess'd!
> No sweeter sounds e'er struck the ear,
> Than when ST. PATRICK silence broke,
> Sweet as the tuneful Harp and clear,

12 Ibid., 15, 18 Aug. 1780.   13 Ibid., 4, 22, 25, 29 Aug. 1780.   14 Ibid., 11 Aug. 1780.

His melting voice as thus he spoke:
"Rous'd by th' inspiring trump of Fame,
Willing I quit the realms of light,
And, hov'ring o'er my Isle proclaim,
'That glorious is the present sight!'
Old Jason with the golden fleece,
First visited your happy shore,
And Pallas left her favourite Greece,
To teach you Wisdom's sacred lore.
From thee the Caledonian race,
Their origin and silence drew,
Altho' they now have not the grace,
To own the debt so justly due.
When arts and learning all lay dead,
Spurn'd by the Vandal, Goth and Hun,
With thee they vig'rous rear'd their head,
And shone resplendent as the sun.
Then with this crosier in my hand,
I bless'd HIBERNIA'S happy swains;
Drove pois'nous reptiles from your land,
While smiling plenty cheer'd the plains.
Fair freedom glow'd in ev'ry breast,
Undaunted courage was your own,
By no restrictive laws oppress'd,
Then Britain was a land unknown.
Superior guile alone was fit,
To introduce a foreign sway;
Dermot and Henry club'd their wit,
Thus fraud, not valour, gain'd the day.

Wretched Ierne! Still confin'd,
Thy artless simple sons abus'd;
Long have I viewed with troubled mind,
Most gross exactions ne'er refus'd.
Ungrateful B———, whom no sense,
Of gratitude or justness find,
Pal'd thee within an iron fence,
And her own wisdom then admir'd.
Vile pimps encreas'd your pension list;
Minions, and catamites, and whores —
'T was I inspired you to resist,
'T was I that form'd you into Corps!

Behold those virtuous bands array'd,
The genuine offspring of my Isle,
A recipe for a Free Trade —
Protecting Heav'n on them smile!
Your native worth resuming now,
Has stamp'd you with immortal fame;
Remotest times to you shall bow,
And hail your virtues with acclaim!
The spirit of the present time,
To future ages will display,
Principles steady, pure, sublime,
And not the 'fashion of a day'.
Be to yourselves but just and true,
Maintain the present system long;
And while you thus yourselves REVIEW,
No power on earth can do you wrong!"
On sounding pinions, disappear'd,
Our holy Patron from my sight;
(?ak'd), and struck with awe, rever'd,
The splendid vision of the night.

HANGOVER

In the aftermath of the 'free trade' victory, the earl of Abercorn, the owner of a large estate (and commensurate political ambitions) in northeast Donegal and west Tyrone, grew uneasy reading newspapers sent to him in London. 'Six weeks ago,' he wrote a friend on 1 February, 'I thought Ireland was going to be happy. But the later accounts breathe so much lunacy (at least from my part of it) that I do not foresee how the nation is to recover its sober senses'.[15] The mischievous might suggest that had 'the nation' not sobered up the Apprentice Boys would now commemorate the siege by parading from gate to gate (not along the top of the walls) while waving Irish flags, knocking back large measures of Bushmills in glasses propped up by potatoes and haggling with street-traders at the back of the walls about the price of their 'Proud to be a Paddy' T-shirts. Bu the nation did recover its 'sober senses': by the 1810s Ribbonmen (who conceived Catholics to be the true Irish) and Orangemen (who thought Protestants inherently superior) were at each others throats across northwest Ulster. Orangeism, however, did not put down deep roots in the region and

15 Abercorn to Arthur Pomeroy, London, 1 Feb. 1780, published in J.H. Gebbie (ed.), *An introduction to the Abercorn letters as relating to Ireland* (Omagh, 1972), p. 331.

liberalism or simply reasonableness remained a central element in Protestant political culture as evidence by the tenant-right politics of the Presbyterian Londonderry Standard in the mid-nineteenth century (James McKnight, the Irish-speaking editor, adopted the level-headed position that 'civil liberty as established by William III has been taken from the people of Ireland by the priests and the landlords'). The pragmatic approach of north Donegal unionists after the provincial leadership dropped them like a hot potato in the 1920s and, most recently, the genuine concern for the whole community displayed by the Apprentice Boys of Derry at a time when the Orange Order by laying siege to the Garvaghy Road was demonstrating yet again the failure of triumph.[16]

16 *Londonderry Standard*, 21 Mar. 1868, quoted in B.M. Walker, *Ulster politics: The formative years*, 1868-86 (Belfast, 1989), p. 37.

'We have a strong city':[1] politicised Protestantism, evangelicalism and the siege myth in early nineteenth-century Derry

Mark McGovern

INTRODUCTION: A 'DISTINCTLY PROTESTANT POLITICAL CULTURE'

A 'distinctly Protestant political culture' emerged in Ireland in the first half of the nineteenth century.[2] Of course, Protestantism had been a significant social and political factor in Irish society before this, but between 1800 and 1850 a very specific Protestant sense of collective identity came to play a major role in Irish political life. The culture associated with the commemoration of the Derry siege was to be deeply affected by these changes. To examine the relationship between Protestantism, this Protestant political culture and the siege myth in Derry during the early nineteenth century it is necessary to explore three elements. First, how the emergence of this politicised Protestantism gave rise to campaigns in defence of the 'Protestant Constitution' that in turn found an avenue of expression through the siege culture. Linked to this is the growth of the 'moral machinery' of early nineteenth-century Protestantism and the influence that Protestant evangelicalism had upon the discursive meaning of the siege mentality. Lastly, these two processes were drawn together in the policy of 'All Protestant Union' that (by the middle of the century) had become a central aspect of the siege myth.

The challenges offered to the power of the Ascendancy through the early nineteenth century were met by what Ian D'Alton has described as 'a specific political Protestantism which used the sectarian bond to create a political identity'.[3] That identity projected the imagery of besiegement as defining the position of the Protestant population. Even in relation to the siege myth this was a significant shift. Perceptions of the Derry siege throughout the eighteenth

---

1 This title is taken from a biblical verse often used in relation to the siege and siege anniversary sermons, Isaiah 26:1: We have a Strong City/ He sets up liberation as walls and bulwark/ Open the gates that the righteous nation/ which keeps the faith may enter in.' 2 Ian D'Alton, *Protestant politics and society in Cork 1812-1844* (Cork, 1980), p. 55. 3 Ibid., p. 225.

century tended to see it as a triumph already achieved, or as one that would be secured in the victory of that most contentious concept 'liberty'.[4] It was a reflection of the relative security and confidence of the 'Protestant political nation' and the limited challenge presented to it by the mass of the population that such a sense of the siege had existed.

However, the radical and revolutionary 1790s and the rise of an insurgent peasantry greatly undermined confidence within the Irish ruling class persuading them (initially with some reluctance) to support the restructuring of colonial authority through the Act of Union. Moreover, despite their undoubted continued influence throughout the century, that sense of confidence was never restored in quite the same way again. Through the drawn-out struggles of the nineteenth century the material domination of the landed aristocracy was broken down while, at the same time, those struggles saw a new pattern of social and political alignments take shape. Such alignments and the formation of new hegemonic political blocs ensured that the 'siege mentality' and the siege myth came more and more to the fore.

What conditioned the growth of this definitively Protestant political culture was the fact that most non-Catholics in Ireland experienced social change as a threat to their social, political and economic position. Undoubtedly this experience was not the same for working, middle and upper class Protestants. Yet the imagery of besiegement could allow Protestant workers, farmers, businessmen and landlords to see their plights as being interwoven and a call to defence as necessitating inter-dependence. Whether real or not the perception of 'threat', and the accompanying language of besiegement, materially affected the attitudes and actions of many Irish Protestants and conditioned the growing consciousness of the 'whole Protestant community' as an 'imagined community' distinct specifically because of religious difference.[5] This was particularly important given the ongoing tensions of inter-Protestant relations. The Derry siege myth was an increasingly crucial component of that worldview and for Derry Protestants in particular the siege emerged as a symbol of a Protestant religiosity that was itself being discursively recast.

It is important to note from the outset that this was clearly not the case for all Irish Protestants whose political loyalties were more diverse than is often assumed. Protestants were very much to the fore in early nationalist movements, in tenant rights agitation and through liberal Presbyterianism a large number vigorously opposed attempts to fuse Protestantism with the politics of Toryism and the Union throughout this period. The radical dissenter impulses

---

4 Mark McGovern, 'The siege myth: the siege of Derry in Ulster Protestant political culture, 1689-1939' (unpublished PhD thesis, University of Liverpool, 1994). 5 Benedict Anderson, *Imagined communities: reflections on the origin and spread of nationalism* (London, 1984); Terence Brown, *The whole Protestant community: the making of a historical myth* (Field Day, Derry, 1985).

that had been so critical to the United Irishmen left a legacy that was to be felt for many years to come within many sections of non-Catholic opinion. Nevertheless, such political alignments were ultimately (and increasingly) more the exception than the rule.

As the siege parades emerged as more firmly established, regularly practised and carefully organised (if still largely localised) affairs in the early nineteenth century these historical processes and social forces would determine the reading of the siege that increasingly prevailed. In doing so the siege myth would also mirror the sectarianised class relations that shaped the public life of the city in this period

'A PROTESTANT CULTURE IN A CATHOLIC CITY': CLASS, ECONOMY
AND SECTARIANISM IN EARLY NINETEENTH-CENTURY DERRY

The increasing importance of both industrial capitalism and market relations in the organisation of agriculture transformed the nature of the Ulster economy and society in the first half of the nineteenth century.[6] The north east of Ireland experienced an industrial revolution unparalleled elsewhere in the island that made Belfast the only truly nineteenth-century industrial city in Ireland. This process of economic change accelerated rapidly from the 1850s onward but had already had a significant impact by the mid-century. While the expansion of Belfast far out-stripped that of Derry, the latter too was deeply affected by the increasingly capitalist organisation and commercial orientation of both the rural and urban economies.

In Derry, however, expansion occurred under very particular circumstances. The economy of the north-west was both relatively autonomous and peripheral. The limited development of both a substantial manufacturing base and build up of local capital had a direct bearing on class relations and the creation of a political environment that was ripe for 'sectarian-orientated political warfare'. In addition, the over-dependence of the local economy on external trade would ensure that local business and landed interests were anything but equivocal in their support for the introduction of the Union in 1800. This would clearly also have a direct bearing on their subsequent emergence as vociferous advocates of the link with Britain and the 'Protestant Constitution'.

Economic growth did ensure the emergence of a growing, if impoverished working class population. Most of these new urban workers were rural

6 Peter Gibbon, *The origins of Ulster unionism: the formation of Protestant popular politics and ideology in nineteenth century Ireland* (Manchester, 1975); Liam Kennedy & P. Ollerenshaw (eds), *An economic history of Ulster 1820-1940* (Manchester, 1985); Brian Mitchel, *The making of Derry: an economic history* (Derry, 1992); Cormac O'Grada, *Ireland: a new economic history: 1780-1939* (Oxford, 1994).

migrants from Donegal where the commercialisation of farming was forcing peasants from the land. What the migrants found in the city was often little better than what had been left behind. The main sources of employment in Derry were the port and the construction industry. Both of these involved high levels of casual and unskilled labour producing a workforce that was under-employed, poorly paid and with little or no security. These conditions created working class communities for whom any economic downturn could have dire consequences.

Overwhelmingly these new migrants were also Catholic. This greatly effected the denominational balance of the Derry population. Through the first half of the nineteenth century the predominantly Protestant population (concentrated in particular within the city walls) was slowly overtaken by a burgeoning Catholic community. By the middle of the century a clear Catholic majority had been established in the city and by 1861, there were 12,036 Catholics and only 8,839 Protestants of various denominations. By the mid-nineteenth century the Protestant culture of the siege existed in a Catholic city.[7]

Most of the Catholic community lived in the Bogside area. The Bogside, located on low-lying and marshy ground in the western shadow of the walled city, had been a site of Catholic settlement since the seventeenth century but in the early 1800s it grew significantly. The city centre, on the other hand, continued to be not only the commercial and administrative centre of the city but also almost wholly Protestant. At the same time the Protestant working class lived mainly in the Fountain area that ran along the eastern city wall. What therefore emerged within the expanding city was a pattern of sectarian, as well as class residential segregation, similar to the system of 'confessional villages' and 'shatter zones' that existed in Belfast. Unlike Belfast, however, the commercial centre of the city was not a 'confessionally indifferent zone', but was confessionally distinct, situated between the two main working class areas and of great symbolic significance. As a result the centre of the city itself became a sort of shatter zone and a regular site of rioting and political demonstrations. Allied to this the ritualistic demonstration of territorial control, that became a feature of Orange marches throughout Ulster (born out of this pattern of segregated settlement), made the walls of the city, not only a metaphor for Protestant power, but also the site for the physical and public demonstration of that power.

---

7 *Census of Ireland, 1861: Province of Ulster, the city and county borough of Londonderry* (Dublin, 1861); Col. R. E. Colby, *Ordnance survey memoir of the County of Londonderry*, vol. 1: *memoir of the city and north western liberties of Londonderry, parish of Templemore* (Dublin, 1837); R. Simpson, *The annals of Derry: showing the rise and progress of the town from the earliest accounts on record to the plantation under King James I and thence of the city of Londonderry to the present time* (Derry, 1847), p.215.

THE 'ELECT' AND THE 'DAMNED': PROTESTANT RELIGIOSITY
IN EARLY NINETEENTH-CENTURY DERRY

The growth of sectarian political warfare was also dependent upon the chang-
ing nature of Protestantism itself that accompanied the onset of the modern.[8]
The rise in fundamentalist religiosity during the 'Second Reformation' in the
1820s and 1830s was driven by the emotive 'conversionist' ethos of 'enthusiastic Protestantism' that would reach its zenith in the Ulster Revival of 1859.
Such Protestantism promoted an 'ethnocentrism' whereby 'holiness was lived
as an external state, accessible to perception and standing in opposition to pro-
fanity' and constructed a view of society divided between the 'elect' and the
'damned'. It therefore implied that those who were not saved did so by choice
and were as a consequence responsible for their non-election. The public man-
ifestation of this division would, in turn, be seen in their actions. This was a
recipe for a sectarianised world view, and one which be could be imagined
through the model of an 'elect besieged' in the siege myth. Revivalism also gave
rise to a growing role for populist evangelical preachers as 'enthusiastic leaders'
who would become an increasing feature of Protestant politics in the middle
and late nineteenth century. Here again the imagery of the siege myth would
provide a model for social action, particularly as the cult of George Walker
provided a suitable icon celebrating the role of the 'pastor-politician'.

Yet as studies of early nineteenth-century Protestantism (and particularly of
Methodism) in English society have noted, the emotive character of religious
evangelicalism was combined with a strict moral code that found 'profane'
emotion abhorrent.[9] Methodism provided outlets for emotional release while,
at the same time, socialising the believer into a strict moral value system. This
was a role shared by the evangelical religiosity of the 'Second Reformation' in
Ireland.[10] A whole series of institutions, activities and attitudes were involved
in the 'Second Reformation', from the educational and bible groups which
sprang up throughout Ireland, to the rise of teetotalism. Indeed Methodism
itself was far from insignificant in Ulster Protestantism during this period, if
always remaining a minority strain. However, the form of religiosity that
Methodism introduced had an impact far beyond the relatively small number

---

8 Peter Gibbon, *The origins of Ulster Unionism;* David Hempton, *Evangelical Protestantism in
Ulster society, 1740-1890* (London, 1992); David Miller, *Queen's rebels: Ulster loyalism in historical
perspective* (Dublin, 1978) pp 80-6, ['Presbyterianism and Modernisation in Ulster', *Past and
present*, 80, August 1978, pp 66-90]. 9 L.L. Shiman, *Crusade against drink in England* (London,
1988); E.P. Thompson, *The making of the English working class* (London, 1963). 10 E. Bryn, *The
Church of Ireland in the age of Catholic Emancipation* (New York, 1982); D. Bowen, *The Protestant
crusade in Ireland, 1800-70: a study of Protestant-Catholic relations between the Act of Union and
Disestablishment* (Dublin, 1978); Sean Connolly, *Religion and society in nineteenth century Ireland*
(Dublin, 1985).

of Methodists in Ulster. It was the stimulus Methodism gave to the wider evangelical movement in which it made its 'most important contribution to Irish Society'.[11]

Certainly the evangelical movement developed strongly in both the Church of Ireland and Dissenter faiths in Derry during the first half of the nineteenth century. As had been the case since the late seventeenth century the Derry Protestant population in the period 1800 to 1850 was made up of around 60% non-Anglicans and 40% members of the Church of Ireland. Consequently both had a significant presence in the city during a period when churches were coming to play an increasing regulatory role in the daily lives of adherents.[12] Not suprisingly, given the place of the Established Church as an organisational foundation of the Ascendancy, it was more influential amongst the local ruling class and the Derry see, as one of the richest in the country, was (in the main) a bastion of conservative interest. In addition, however, the congregation of the First Derry Presbyterian Meeting House also included a large proportion of the mercantile class who were relatively well integrated with the local Episcopalian elite. The ministers of the First Derry congregation provided local Presbyterianism with its leadership and several were influential figures within the synod of Ulster. Both Protestant denominations were therefore catered for by well-established, well-funded and well-placed ecclesiastical structures.

In addition the wave of religious enthusiasm that accompanied the expansion of the city increased the physical and social presence of Protestantism locally. Two Methodist chapels had been established by the 1830s and also ran very active bible societies. The early nineteenth century saw the formation of numerous Protestant bible and missionary societies that provided the main organisational impetus of religious revivalism in the 1820s and 1830s. Most of these societies had branches in Derry including the 'Association for Discounting Vice', the 'Hibernian Society', the 'Church Missionary Society' and a small proselytising organisation called the 'Londonderry auxiliary to the Irish Society for the promoting the education of the native Irish through the medium of their own language'. Their central aim was the propagation of evangelical Protestantism amongst the working class. For example, most evangelical bodies were based in the Fountain and when the Episcopalian bishop of Derry encouraged the construction of the Free Church in Great James Street in 1830 it was specifically designed for the 'convenience of the working classes'.[13]

There was also a significant expansion of a Presbyterian presence in the city.

11 David Hempton,'Methodism in Irish Society, 1770-1830', *Transactions of the Royal Historical Society*, 5th Series, 36 (1986), pp 117-42. 12 Col. R.E. Colby, *Ordnance survey memoir of Londonderry*, pp 190-1. 13 Ibid, pp 147-55; W.S. Ferguson, *Ulster architectural heritage society historic buildings, groups of buildings, areas of architectural importance in and near the city of Derry* (Belfast, 1970), pp 16-27; John Hempton, *The siege and history of Londonderry* (Derry, 1861); R. Simpson, *Annals of Derry*, p. 230.

The First Derry Presbyterian Meeting House was joined by the 'Scotch Church' built in Great James Street in 1837. One of the schismatic strands of Ulster Presbyterianism, the Seceders, had found a meeting house in Fountain Street in 1783 and was joined by a second Seceder congregation in the late 1830s. This brand of Presbyterianism was both 'evangelical and orthodox' in character and it was the increasingly evangelical orientation of the Ulster synod that encouraged the union of the Ulster and Seceder synods in the formation of the General Assembly in 1840, producing four mainstream Presbyterian congregations in Derry by the middle of the century. In addition there was a Covenanters Meeting House, again situated in Fountain Street, built in 1810, with a second founded in the Waterside in the late 1840s.

The Sunday school movement also had a growing presence and a 'Londonderry Sunday School Union' was established in 1832 whose main aim was the 'communicating of scriptural instruction' and which had as many as 2,500 pupils enrolled within two years. Significantly the rules of the Union suggest an avowedly conversionist approach as it denied entry to anyone who held 'professedly Arian or Socinian principles'. By the 1830s Arianism was closely identified both with Old Light, or intellectualist, Presbyterianism and with anti-Tory politics. Arianism was, however, little in evidence among the various Presbyterian organisations in Derry.

The extent of interest in Protestantism can also be judged from the popularity of religious publications. In 1834 a list of the most widely sold publications in Derry was topped by the *Orthodox Presbyterian* and the *Christian Freeman*, the journals of the synod of Ulster and the Seceders respectively. Similarly by the 1830s it was estimated that approximately 50% of Episcopalians and 35% of Presbyterians attended religious services every week in the three Church of Ireland, two Methodist and five Presbyterian places of worship then established in Derry. The congregations of all the Protestant churches were on the increase as, it would seem, was the influence of Protestantism in the lives of Derry Protestants.[14]

FIGHTING FOR THE 'PROTESTANT CONSTITUTION':
THE SIEGE PARADES AND THE FOUNDING OF THE
APPRENTICE BOYS, 1800-1835

In the thirty years between the 1798 Rebellion and the introduction of Catholic Emancipation the dominant conservative sections of the Protestant ruling class saw themselves principally in the guise of the defenders of the 'Protestant Constitution'. In Derry, the phrase the 'Protestant Constitution' was faithfully

14 Ibid., pp 149-1.

conjured up for approbation at every public gathering in which elements of the ruling class took part and really came to mean the same thing as the power and prestige of the local corporate order. Nor did the granting of Catholic political rights in 1829 dismantle this perception, for, while the phrase itself largely disappeared, the identification of the establishment with Protestantism was, if anything, intensified. It was a potent political slogan because the existing constitutional arrangement did indeed legitimate the distinctly Protestant structure of social authority that prevailed in Derry as elsewhere in Ireland and combined with the economic interests of a mercantile class that increasingly saw its interests tied to those of British capitalism and the empire. During the first decades of the nineteenth century the siege parades became a ritualised and public means of manifesting this 'fight' for the Protestant Constitution.

Locally the struggle over the continuation of Protestant political supremacy was made all the more relevant by the rising Catholic population. These demographic changes were even more important as the early decades of the century witnessed the rise of a new kind of politics. Organised, popular, mass campaigns, in support of Catholic demands for more equitable civil and political treatment represented a new form of political mobilisation. These campaigns culminated in the winning of Catholic emancipation in 1829 and helped to create a political consciousness amongst the Irish Catholic population that had profound political repercussions. In Derry the rise of this new political consciousness, combined with the growing size of the Catholic community, produced a challenge to the local Protestant establishment and the conservatism of the local Catholic political and clerical leadership.

The rise in antagonism amongst Catholics to the siege parades, evident from the first decade of the century onward, was born out of this new consciousness and Catholic working class rejection of political submissiveness. The first outbreak of rioting during the siege parades occurred as early as 1809. The same year saw the emergence of both O'Connellite political activity and the re-emergence of Ribbonism in the Derry area. By the 1830s the local Catholic population was willing, and able, to physically oppose the public demonstration of Protestant supremacy, through the siege culture, with some success. Increasingly, then, Derry Catholics saw the siege parades as the cultural performance of their own disempowerment. While advocates of the siege culture disavowed this intention the fact that the parade celebrated a political structure and corporate regime where the exclusion of Catholics was a fundamental basis of power and that, more and more, the parades incorporated the symbolism of Orangeism, made such claims sound, at least to Derry Catholic ears, more than a little hollow. There was a coarse political logic to the siege parades as a display of Catholic disempowerment. The mercantile elite derived much of their political authority from the support of city freemen, who were exclusively Protestant. The main political goal of the local ruing Protestant interest was therefore to secure and maintain local systems of patronage, which rested upon the continued exclusion of Catholics.

It was against this background that, through the early decades of the nine-teenth century, the siege parades became firmly established as annual events. From the end of the 1790s the figure and influence of that bastion of Ascendancy interest, Sir George Hill, had profoundly influenced the parades. Hill was the dominant political force in the North West in this period and took a leading part in the siege parades as they became increasingly conservative and sectarian in outlook. From 1800 onward the parades were organised by Hill as commander of the local yeomanry. Indeed the yeomanry became so identified with the siege culture that by 1814 they were referred to as 'the modern Apprentice Boys'. Numbering anything up to 400 men (and often accompanied by regular army regiments) the Yeomanry marched, fired volleys and ritually closed the gates of the city on 12 December each year.[15]

It is not insignificant that this period also saw the route of the siege parades include (for the first time in 1808, the year of the first clashes) a full circuit of the walls, which meant that at one point the marchers looked down upon the Bogside from the Royal Bastion.[16] Showing control of the walls through marching around them became a way of demonstrating a belief that Protestant power still held sway in the city and that even if the Catholic community 'with-out' was expanding rapidly, privilege would continue to be held by those 'within'. The parades were, in addition, becoming simply more visible to the Catholic population of the Bogside.

If the intention of such displays was to symbolise the power of the estab-lishment and their exercise of authority via the rule of law, this was nowhere better demonstrated than in December 1813.[17] In the midst of what was a politically tense period, the 'shutting of the Gates' anniversary was marked by a more substantial parade than usual and was used as the occasion for laying the foundation stone of the new courthouse. The whole event emphasised the power of the local elite and identified it with symbols of Orangeism. Indeed the symbols and culture of Orangeism had become totally enmeshed in the siege practices as a report of a parade of 1814 illustrates: 'An Orange Flag, having the figure of KING WILLIAM on horseback, was seen waving majestically from the steeple, while the Virgin Flag graced the eastern battlement of the church. Above each of the principle gates was painted in large capitals on an Orange background: NO SURRENDER 1688'.[18] In 1813 the Corporation had actually re-named the Diamond, 'King William's Square', though they were forced to revert to the original title by the Irish Society in 1819.[19]

15 *Londonderry Journal*, 20 Dec. 1814. 16 John Hempton, *siege and history of Londonderry*, p. 437. 17 *Londonderry Journal*, 19 Dec. 1813. 18 Ibid., 20 Dec. 1814. 19 T.H. Mullin, *Ulster's historical city: Derry/Londonderry* (Coleraine, 1986), p. 140.

The Revd John Graham (the cleric who, more than any other, was involved with the promotion of the siege culture) regularly joined Hill at the head of the siege processions riding a white horse. The figure of a white horse had become synonymous with the cult of William, blending the political significance of a militarily powerful establishment, personified by William, with the biblical imagery of Christ the saviour astride the 'pale horse of Revelations'.[20] From the beginning of the century the siege parades had therefore become occasions for demonstrating the prestige of the Ascendancy, and by the second decade of the century that prestige, the symbolism of Orangeism and of the siege were inextricably bound up together.

The political significance of this was not lost on contemporaries and particularly on the expanding Catholic population. Such an identification of the parades with politicised Protestantism coincided with a period of growing Catholic political and agrarian agitation, emphasised by the militancy of local Ribbonism brought into the city by the new rural migrants. In addition a Catholic Committee was established in the city and in September 1811 a large demonstration was held in support of O'Connell. Notably the Relief parade in August that year saw a major row break out over the wearing of Orange ribbons by the yeomanry. Seven Catholic members of the Londonderry Legion left the ranks during the parade as a protest when others 'appeared with Orange lilies in their caps'. George Hill would argue that wearing Orange lilies was 'actuated solely by a desire to commemorate the day in the usual manner, without any regard to religion or party' and that Catholics (far from finding offence in the wearing of lilies) had occasion to do so themselves and that the practice was well-established long before the formation of the Orange Order.[21] Yet it is clear that the perception of political neutrality was not one shared by all and that even some of those involved with the Yeomanry were concerned enough about the political implications of wearing Orange lilies that they were willing to disobey orders. It is also clear that whatever meaning may or may not have been given to the wearing of an Orange lily in the past it was an increasingly contentious political symbol by the second decade of the nineteenth century.

Between 1812 and 1815 tensions and clashes surrounding the siege demonstrations intensified, in part due to an intensification of political differences within the Catholic community. These came to focus on a dispute between the conservative local bishop 'Orange-Charlie' O'Donnell and Fr Cornelius O'Mullan, a local priest active on the Catholic Committee and with strong support within local Ribbonism. This culminated in a heated meeting held in

20 Belinda Loftus, *Mirrors: William III and mother Ireland* (Dublin, 1990), pp 22-30; Cecil D. Milligan, *Browning memorial window souvenir: Browning memorial with a short historical note on the rise and progress of the Apprentice Boys of Derry clubs* (Derry, 1952), p. 11; Tom Paulin, *Ireland and the English crisis* (Newcastle, 1984), p. 171. 21 John Hempton, *siege and history of Londonderry*, pp 440-1.

the Long Tower Church in November 1813 when O'Mullan, backed by a number of armed Ribbonmen ejected O'Donnell. After this O'Mullan gave a speech denouncing the corporation as Orangemen, and the bishop as an 'Orange-Papist'. O'Mullan was subsequently excommunicated, arrested, tried by Hill and sentenced to one month in prison for incitement to riot and assault.[22] At the trial Hill argued that O'Mullan was wrong to have implied that the corporation was Orange, and again used the case of the siege parades to make his point arguing that 'in the Yeomanry Corps, which I have the honour to command . . . of which not one-tenth were Roman Catholics, we have forborne for the last three years, on the Ist of August, the anniversary of the Relief of Derry, to exhibit the Orange lily. . .out of respect to the feelings of our Roman Catholic Brethren, then for the first time expressed'.[23]

Yet the Diamond had been renamed after William that same year, a month later the 'principal citizens' attended the December parade 'decorated with Orange ribbons' and in 1814 an 'Orange Flag, having the figure of King William' flew from the cathedral steeple, a feature which was regularly repeated in the next few years. Similarly, the then very much pro-Protestant *Journal* provides an insight into whether or not the parades were as politically neutral as Hill sought to suggest: 'The silly cant of a mistaken liberality, which for a time usurped the seat of reason, and considered all regard for established customs and opinions as uncharitable and criminal attached odium even to the very colours under which our deliverer bled for liberty. Of late however it has been happily discovered that the enemies to the commemoration of the event which secured our country's freedom are also the enemies of the state.'[24] To oppose the parades was, in other words, to be an enemy of the state because the guarantee against 'civil and religious liberty being trampled on by ignorance and superstition' was the Protestant Constitution, which the siege had come to symbolise.

After this initial period of conflict over the siege anniversaries things returned to a relative calm until the early 1820s. In 1822, however, there was a full-scale confrontation over the siege parades that involved not only communal conflict, but also for the first time, friction between Derry Protestants and forces of the state. Several factors led to this situation. A wave of political and social unrest was evident throughout the country with both a resurgence of Ribbon activities and the emergence O'Connellite campaigning on an unprecedented scale. Government policy had also shifted, adopting a more conciliatory line toward Catholic grievances. In Dublin, this situation led to serious riots on

22 *Londonderry Journal*, 9 Nov. 1813; *Dublin Evening Post*, 29 Jan. 1814; M.R. O'Connell (ed.), *The correspondence of Daniel O'Connell*, vol. 3 (Dublin, 1972) p. 96; Revd J. Graham: *Derriana: consisting of a history of the siege of Londonderry and the defence of Enniskillen in 1688 and 1689, with historical poetry and biographical notes* (Derry, 1883) pp 157-62. 23 John Hempton, *siege and history of Londonderry*, p. 442. 24 *Londonderry Journal*, 20 Dec. 1814.

12 July 1822 and the banning of Orange demonstrations to the statue of William in College Green thereafter.[25]

The change in state policy had already been signalled in Derry by the decision of the local regular army commander to prevent both the military, and the Yeomanry, from taking part in the 'Closing of the Gates' parade in 1821.[26] As a consequence an 'Apprentice Boys' society was formed to carry out the various practices previously performed by the army. This was an important departure. Although there is some evidence that an Apprentice Boys Club was formed in 1814, from which the modern association dates its foundation, it is from 1821 that a definite record exists and an account of the August parade of 1822 significantly made a distinction between 'the loyal Apprentice Boys and the Londonderry legion', which had previously tended to be regarded as the same thing.[27]

During the Relief parade in 1822 a riot broke out between a Catholic crowd and the marchers; a conflict continued several weeks later at the Derry race meeting, a traditional occasion of feud and faction fighting. At a meeting held on the evening of 1 August 1822, the Revd John Graham suggested that the siege was commemorated 'fearing God, honouring the King' and spoke against the mooted restrictions to be placed upon Orange parades.[28] The direction of state policy from the mid-1820s onward had a demonstrably alienating impact on the most committed advocates of the siege culture. Graham, whom one contemporary described as a man of 'somewhat eccentric habits, simple, honest and devotedly loyal', was also recorded as the Grand Master of the Londonderry County Orange Lodge in 1835.[29] As early as December 1822 he was criticising government restrictions placed on certain Orange activities at the siege anniversaries. In a poem, written in the same month, Graham argued that although the founders of Derry had 'Orange (as) their banner, True-blue their heart', the story of the siege also provided a cautionary tale against the possibility of betrayal on the part of those in authority,

25 Jacqueline Hill,'National festivals, the State and Protestant Ascendancy in Ireland, 1790-1829', *Irish Historical Studies* 24/3, pp 46-7. **26** John Hempton, *siege and history of Londonderry*, p. 446. **27** *Londonderry Journal*, 13 Aug. 1822. The record of a club being formed in 1814 comes from a commemorative medal struck in 1889 for the bicentennial of the siege relief that dates the founding of the Apprentice Boys from that date, see M. Milligan, 'The rise and progress of the Apprentice Boys of Derry association: a century old prophecy that remains unfulfilled' (unpublished, no date); Cecil D. Milligan, *The Walker Club centenary: a history of the Apprentice Boys of Derry and biographical notes on Governor Walker* (Derry, 1947) p. 21. **28** John Graham, *Derriana* p. 157. **29** *First report from the select committee appointed to inquire into the nature, character, extent and tendency of the Orange Lodges, Associations or Societies, in Ireland*, House of Commons, vol. 2, 1835, p. 43; Revd A. Dawson, *George Walker, the siege of Derry* (Belfast, 1887), p. 34.

At length in time this little town grows great,
Procures bad rulers, men affecting state
Practise vile measures, Govern as they please,
Refuse no bribe, and still they live at ease,
E'en seel the city for love of fees. . .
Itching for gain their Country's rights forgo,
City's, nay states, they'd barter with a foe,
Even lay religion and her honour low.[30]

Such sentiments anticipated the growing distance that emerged between the state and the Orange Order over the following decade. In 1825 the Grand Lodge of Ireland was suspended, in 1832 the Anti-Processions Act was introduced and the Grand Lodge was actually dissolved in 1836. The Order became more populist from the early 1820s, the focus of its grass roots activists fell upon the preservation of their public display of power through their 'right to march'. For the upper class leadership concern was centred on preserving the 'Protestant constitution'. The desire to promote this politicised Protestantism (and growing official censure of the same) led to the establishment of other hard-line Protestant bodies in the late 1820s, foremost among them were the 'Brunswick clubs', created to lead opposition to the emancipation campaign in 1828.[31]

Opposition to the prospect of Catholic Emancipation was undoubtedly widespread amongst Derry Protestants. When, for example, the owner of the *Journal* decided to support the introduction of Emancipation it caused the editor to leave to establish an alternative paper, the *Londonderry Sentinel*, whose principles were avowedly ultra-Protestant. The circulation of the *Sentinel* was soon almost double that of the (now renamed) *Derry Journal*. Yet, divisions within the personnel of the Derry Protestant elite that followed the declaration of support for emancipation of the local MP, G.R. Dawson, left them unable to a cohesive campaign during 1828-9.[32]

However, the Orange movement certainly had a strong presence within the city and the establishment of several societies of 'Apprentice Boys' in Derry during the late 1820s and the early 1830s needs to be seen in the context of this conflict over the nature and role of Orangeism, its increasing popularisation and the emphasis of its working class members upon their 'traditional' marching rights. A 'No Surrender Apprentice Boys club' was formed in October 1824 and by 1832 this (and another 'No Surrender club') were joined by what the *Ordnance Survey* called the 'Death and Glory club' which was 'chiefly

30 Ibid. 31 Revd M. W Dewar. *Orangeism: a new historical appreciation* (Belfast, 1967), pp 111-130; Tony Gray, *The Orange Order* (London, 1972) pp 97-118. 32 Brian Lacey, *Siege City: the story of Derry and Londonderry* (Belfast, 1990) p. 173.

composed of journeymen tradesmen'.[33] From the late 1820s it was these various Apprentice Boys clubs that were the main organisers of the siege parades, ensuring that the various rituals and practices of the siege culture continued to be a central element of political activity.

By the late 1820s the overtly Protestant definition of the parades was also clearly signalled by the growing emphasis on the role of George Walker. Walker was the 'warrior-priest' of the siege myth. While Walker had always figured as a hero-icon of the siege his elevated and venerated status from the 1820s onward was due to the growing importance of Protestantism as such within the siege culture. This was emphasised by the construction of Walker's Pillar, commissioned by the Apprentice Boys and completed by August 1828. The statue of Walker, sited on the Royal Bastion, towered over the Bogside and depicted Walker in clerical garb with a sword tied around his waist, one hand outstretched toward the Foyle and the other holding an open bible with 'Exodus 20' written upon it. It was an icon of Protestant power and the imagined deliverance of the 'chosen people'.[34]

The statue was completed amid an atmosphere of increasing sectarian tension, against a background of local political and economic turmoil, that stimulated the regular appearance (for the first time in the city) of popular Catholic marches. From 1830 onward there was a Catholic St Patrick's day parade that marched around the outside base of the walls emphasising the fact that the symbolism of the walls as a sign of territorial control and power was one understood by all concerned. Matters came to a head in early 1832.[35] A corporation ban imposed on parades prevented a Catholic St Patrick's Day march taking place but also elicited a public declaration from the (Orange linked) mayor, Joshua Gillespie that future Protestant marches would also be prevented. As a result (and following the introduction of the Anti-Procession Act in August 1832) the Relief parade that summer was considerably modified. However, the following December saw an election defeat for the pro-Emancipation Dawson and victory for R. A. Ferguson, the new dominant force in Derry politics. The election led to scuffles and as Ferguson was 'chaired' an effigy of Lundy was taken from the corporation hall, in direct contravention both of the ban imposed by the mayor and the Anti-Procession Act, and burnt for the first time on Walker's Pillar.[36]

While several Apprentice Boys were subsequently prosecuted, Catholic anger over the failure of the city authorities to prevent such displays led to protracted struggles over parades between 1833 and 1835. By 1836 an effective

33 Col. R.E. Colby, *Ordnance survey*, p. 198, John Hempton, *siege and history of Londonderry*, p. 449. 34 Ibid., pp 119-20; W. S. Ferguson, *Architectural history of Derry*, p. 12; Cecil D. Milligan, *Centenary of the Walker Club*, pp. 72-4. 35 D. Derry Murphy, *Donegal and modern Ulster 1790-1921* (Derry, 1981) p. 45. 36 *Londonderry Journal*, 25 Dec. 1832; John Hempton, *siege and history of Londonderry*, p. 195.

imposition of the Anti-Procession Act had been established and although the
siege anniversaries were marked by a small march to the cathedral the deeply
contentious route around the walls was briefly curtailed. Yet the parades were
to re-emerge in the 1840s with both the wall route and the burning of the effigy
from Walker's Pillar re-established and the Apprentice Boys clubs continued to
exist (and march) throughout the period. However, the mid-1830s marked a
point at which the siege parades (like the Orange marches) had become socially
disruptive that the state authorities, and even to some extent the local elite,
viewed them as counter-productive to the maintenance of order and the status
quo.

     Throughout the preceding thirty years the siege practices had become
marked by an essentially 'Protestant' political orientation that was both, in
large part, conservative and founded upon attachment to the British link. The
full force of the local Ascendancy had conditioned the growth of the siege culture in the aftermath of the 1798 Rebellion and the Act of Union and this continued to be a dominant influence. The presence of members of the
Corporation in the parades was apparent until the mid-1830s. The
Corporation hall was used as the site for burning the Lundy effigy until 1835
and R.A. Ferguson continued to patronise the Apprentice Boys clubs throughout the 1830s, 1840s and 1850s. Popular working class involvement notably
grew from the mid-1820s as Orangeism found itself estranged from the state
authorities. In many ways that estrangement reached a peak in the 1830s when
the level of social conflict surrounding the parades had reached such a point
that the corporation was forced to curb the most contentious practices. Most
of those practices were, however, soon to re-appear.

     The whole period from 1800 to 1835 witnessed the growing identification of
the siege as the cultural practice of politicised Protestantism. In a situation
where the Catholic population was growing rapidly, and was itself becoming
more politicised, the public demonstration of this political Protestant identity
became increasingly contentious. As a result the siege culture emerged as the
major focus for the periodic communal conflict that erupted in the city and the
various Apprentice Boys clubs, which appeared in the first decades of the century, were set up and run by the Orange supporters by the 'Protestant
Constitution'.

MORALITY, SOBRIETY AND MYTH: THE SIEGE MYTH AND
EVANGELICALISM, 1830-1850

The growth of the evangelical movement deeply affected the message of the
siege myth. The siege story proved an attractive cultural model to evangelicals.
That attraction lay in two aspects of the siege's symbolic construction. The
siege myth was a 'structure of opposites', a story of a 'besieged' Protestant

population 'inside the walls' could be construed as the 'good' or 'godly' community standing in moral and spiritual, as well as physical, contrast to the 'other', the 'threatening' Catholic 'without'. This was a rich vein of imagery for evangelicals committed to a conception of religiosity that drew a sharp distinction between the 'saved' and the 'damned'.[37]

Just as attractive to Evangelicals was the narrative development of the myth, with its 'sacrificial ethos', its story of a community, faced with a challenge or threat, transported through sacrifice and trial, to salvation or 'Relief'. In this the story of the siege followed a classic mythological structure that 'transforms the determinist world in which we live into a magical world'.[38] The transformation, in this case, involved the passage of the individual religious devotee, psychologically released from a rationally defined social existence through conversion into a state of grace. In this sense, the siege narrative could act as a cultural model for the imagined spiritual biography of the individual evangelical.

At the same time evangelicalism helped usher in the growing routinisation of social life, a form of social puritanism that reflected the onset of modernity. Modern capitalism acquired 'rational structures of law and administration' and the growth of institutional forums for municipal, judicial, medical, educational and social provision. The need to view the external world both rationally and consistently explicable (the basic ideological framework of modernity) led to the apparently paradoxical emphasis on a form of Protestantism that emphasised the internal emotional experience of spirituality. Advocates of Evangelical religion would at the same time, however, call for rationally-structured regulatory organisations that could establish a clear framework of social norms.[39]

The siege culture was deeply affected by the growing importance of the evangelical lobbying Derry. This was evident in several ways. At the most obvious level the promotion of a proselytising Protestant religiosity tended to aggravate sectarian tensions within the city and around the siege marches. But evangelicalism also encouraged the routinisation and social puritanism of the Apprentice Boys clubs, particularly from the 1840s onward. The siege anniversaries had always been accompanied by a large degree of festive, and often raucous, behaviour typified by the 'Bottle and Glass parties' that were a dominant feature of their early development. Such activities increasingly became

37 Anthony Buckley & Mary Kenny, *Negotiating identity: rhetoric, metaphor and social drama* (Washington D.C., 1995); Jennifer Todd, 'Two traditions in unionist political culture', *Irish Political Studies*, pp 1-26.   38 Richard Kearney, *Transitions: narratives in modern Irish culture* (Manchester, 1988) p. 223.   39 Frank Burton, 'Ideological social relations in Northern Ireland', *British Journal of Sociology*, 30/1 (March 1979), pp 61-80; Peter Gibbon, *The origins of Ulster unionism*; Frank Wright, 'Protestant ideology and politics in Ulster', *European Journal of Sociology*, 14/2 (1971), pp 213-80; Max Weber, *The Protestant ethic and the spirit of capitalism* (London, 1984).

the target for the moral strictures of fundamentalists. By the end of the 1850s such gatherings were being replaced by 'tea parties'. These changes in the culture that surrounded the siege anniversaries reflected the way a particular brand of Protestantism, and a particular moral value system, was inculcated as the communal norm. Prudish morality, and sobriety became markers of identity with the rise of Evangelicalism.

Certainly the upsurge of interest in Protestantism fed into the growing tension in the evident in the confrontations over the siege parades in the 1820s and 1830s. At times the activities of evangelical groups directly caused riots. An influx of itinerant preachers who arrived in the city in 1826 led to several small-scale clashes and a wave of complaints from the local Catholic community against their proselytising activities. This dispute continued through until 1828, when the arrival of two members of the Reformation Society led to the 'Derry Discussion', an unprecedented public clerical debate that was followed by a tacit agreement limiting cross-communal proselytising.[40]

Evangelicalism was, however, more important an influence on the siege parades because it encouraged the growth both of social puritanism and of the regulatory control over various aspects of peoples lives in the city. A major target for evangelicals was what they regarded as the 'social evil' of alcohol and of secular entertainment. The Temperance movement was one of the clearest manifestations of the drive to impose social control over working class lives in particular. During the 1820s the power of this lobby was so great that they conducted several successful campaigns to curb a variety of social activities. In 1837 the *Ordnance Survey* described a 'gravity of character' as the 'most striking feature of the inhabitants of Derry'. This was apparent in 'the repose of the inhabitants rarely disturbed by the noise of the drunken brawler . . . [and a] . . . prevailing indifference to public amusements'. The theatre had recently been closed, concerts had been 'discontinued', the 'coteries presided over by a King and Queen of the Night have died away' and the local horse races had been suspended because they were considered 'injurious to morality'. These developments were ascribed to the 'absorbing influence of political as well as of religious enthusiasm'.[41]

The siege celebrations therefore became one of the few occasions when a large degree social licence was allowed and it may be not unconnected that the extent of ritualised regalia surrounding the marches noticeably increased during the 1820s and 1830s. Far greater use of music, banners and flags, the parading and firing of small canons, the wearing of particular forms of dress, all evidenced a heightening of the theatricality of the events. The consumption of

40 F. Campbell & W. Wallen, *Authenticated report of the discussion which took place between six Roman Catholic priests and six clergymen of the established church in the diocese of Derry, March 1828* (Dublin, 1828).   41 Col. R. E. Colby, *Ordnance survey*, p. 195.

alcohol was also a conspicuous part of the social activity on the demonstrations. This was, however, far from a new aspect of the culture. From the late eighteenth onward 'Bottle and Glass Parties' were held on the siege anniversaries. At a siege 'Bottle and Glass' party in 1832, attended by almost all the gentry and 'leading citizenry' the Corporation Hall was described as being filled to the point of 'suffocation'. Every man brought his own 'bottle and glass' and numerous toasts were drunk to the 'Orange and Blue', 'Rule Britannia'; 'the Protestant Boys' and 'Croppies Lie Down'.[42] Similar in character to the Orange meetings held during the same period these events often went on into the early hours of the morning. Similarly the painting *Burning the Effigy of Lundy in Derry*, produced by an unknown artist at more or less the same time illustrates the 'rough behaviour' or popular culture dimension of the siege culture. Aside from its directly political implications the burning of the Lundy effigy had also emerged as the most carnivalesque of the siege practices.[43]

However, in the 1830s and 1840s the clubs and activities of the siege culture became more and more carefully regulated. Rules were introduced governing the proceedings of the various clubs and ever more stringent guidelines for the conduct of the parades. The organisational character of the clubs changed substantially over these years. While there was a high turnover of clubs forming and dissolving through the 1840s, two were established on a much firmer footing, the Walker Club in 1844, and Murray Club in 1847. The Murray club laid down rules governing the behaviour of its members 'at all times, but more especially on our anniversaries [that], every member shall conduct himself soberly and orderly and shall with all due respect obey the proper commands of his officers, and any member conducting himself irregularly or being drunk and incapable of duty on any such days shall be by the officers deprived of wearing any colours connected with our celebrations'.[44] The organisation of the parades was also becoming more controlled. Meetings were held between the clubs to decide on the form of the siege rituals, a regular order of the clubs in the processions was established and rules were laid down concerning the firing of volleys and the small cannons, which several of the clubs now owned. Similarly a code of dress was established.

This control did have its limits. In the 1840s the popular, 'rough', dimension of the siege parades continued to have a part to play in the activities of the Apprentice Boys clubs. The Murray Club was described in 1849 as a 'youthful band of celebrators' and had passed a resolution the year before to 'hold our Bottle and Glass in company with the No Surrender Club'. However, six years later, even though the 'Bottle and Glass' parties were still continuing at least

42 *Londonderry Sentinel*, 22 Dec. 1832. 43 E. P. Thompson, *Customs in common* (London, 1991); the painting 'Burning the Effigy of Lundy in Derry' is currently housed in the Ulster Museum. 44 Cecil D. Milligan, *The Murray Club centenary, 1847-1947* (Derry, 1947), p. 6.

one club member was 'reprimanded for being intoxicated on the anniversary of the relief'.[45] Certainly the moral climate surrounding the organised siege practices was increasingly imbued with the ethos of mid-Victorian 'respectability', in which teetotalism was very the fore. By the end of the 1850s this drive for social puritanism and sobriety had clearly established an influence on the siege celebrations. In 1858 the Relief parade sermon was preached by the Revd George Steen (a close friend and confidante of Henry Cooke) who described the Apprentice Boys of 1689 as 'men of self-denial who should not be remembered in the wine cup but in our closets and on our knees . . . They have set you an example of moral courage'.[46]

The 1859 revival the following year was the high point of fundamentalist hysteria in nineteenth-century Ulster and a drive against alcohol was one of its central concerns.[47] In Derry one of the two main advocates of the revival was an evangelical Presbyterian minister called Thomas Witherow who would subsequently published an account of the siege of Derry and edited Ash's Diary for its first publication. Through the summer of 1859 huge open air services attended by thousands were held almost every evening in Derry and devotees were reported as being 'stricken' and falling into an hysteria-induced paralysis. Numbers at religious services dramatically increased and the walls of the city were covered with placards with biblical motifs and texts. The impact of revivalism finally established temperance practices as the behavioural norm for the siege culture; at least within what had increasingly become the polite, middle class 'respectable' circles of the Apprentice Boys clubs. In 1861 John Hempton, a leading figure in the Apprentice Boys movement, noted at the Shutting the Gates soirée; 'the progress of the times has changed the customs of our society and instead of the jovial bottle and glass of our predecessors, we now have this tea meeting'.[48]

RAPING THE MAIDEN CITY: SPIRITUALITY AND THE
REPRESENTATION OF GENDER AND COMMUNITY IN
THE SIEGE MYTH, 1830-1850

Temperance was one of the most obvious ways that the values of enthusiastic Protestantism was lived as an 'external state'. The evangelical moral value system of which sobriety was a part, was dramatised in evangelical texts through the imagery of a spiritual life which was beset by a constant struggle waged

45 Ibid., pp 20-2. 46 *Derry Standard*, 17 Aug. 1858. 47 Peter Gibbon *Origins of Ulster unionism*; C. W. Gordon, *The Fifty-nine revival, lest we forget: the wonders of Ulster in 1859* (Belfast, 1949); Revd T. Witherow *Derry and Enniskillen in the year 1689* (Belfast, 1873); *Two diaries of Derry in 1689, being Richard's diary of the fleet and Ash's journal of the siege* (Derry, 1888). 48 *Londonderry Guardian*, 24 Dec. 1861.

between good and evil that demanded sacrifices of the devotee before salvation could be attained. Here again the Deny siege proved a source of inspiration, and a reference point, to numerous early nineteenth century Protestant clerics and evangelicals. This is particularly evident in much of the poetry, songs and fiction of the siege in this period and through which a number of moral strands were together.

The Revd John Graham, the writer of several of the most popular songs relating to the siege regularly employed the imagery of besiegement in his work as a means to entwine the elements of spiritual renewal with sectarian politics and linked these to a 'blood sacrificial ethos and that most Victorian of virtues, 'duty'.[49] These elements were often symbolised in the imagery of the 'Derry Walls' themselves. Indeed the walls of Derry often appear in early nineteenth century Protestant rhetoric not only as a symbol of the collective boundary but also as a metaphor of the individual soul. Similarly, links were increasingly made between the cultural narrative of the siege and the prevailing norms of sexual morality, through the metaphor of the 'Maiden' City. For example, the popular love song *A Maiden Pined by Derry's Walls* emphasised the role of women as lover, wife and mother, and linked this imagery to anti-Catholic sentiment. In similar vein John Graham, in his poem *Derriana* welded the model of the siege, through the motif of maidenhood, to a blend of sacrificial imagery and feminine sexual symbolism.

The use of the walls of Derry as a comforting feminine icon has parallels with (what E.P. Thompson described as) the 'womb-regressive' imagery of many early Methodist hymns and writings.[50] As Thompson argues, the prevalence of such images, linked as they often were to blood-symbolism, promoted sexual repression, a denial of the physical world and encouraged a fixation with death.[51] One of the real powers of such symbolic representation was the ability to fuse several ideological elements together and relate them at one and the same time. The 'virgin' and 'maiden' imagery linked to the siege could therefore establish a definition of gender power relations and the norms of sexual morality as an intrinsic element of a religio-political world-view and an identity of the community.

This is, perhaps, best illustrated in the works on the siege by the English evangelical writer Charlotte Elizabeth.[52] Elizabeth was the author of *The siege*

49 Revd John Graham, *Historical poetry with biographical notes* (Derry, 1822); *Derriana*; *The Orange Lark and other songs of the Orange tradition* (Lurgan, 1983).   **50** E. P. Thomson, *The making of the English working class*, pp 406-11.   **51** Certainly Graham, who often wrote of death as a form of release, revelled in the somewhat macabre re-internment of Walker's bones in 1838 when he dramatically drew his sword at the graveside to lay it upon the skull then being placed into the grave, and according to a witness at the time 'exclaimed in a voice of intense fervour, "now I have done what King James and all his army could not do"': Revd A. Dawson, *George Walker*, p. 34.   **52** Sam Burnside 'No temporising with the foe', *Linen Hall Review*, August

of Derry: A tale of the revolution in 1688 published in the mid-1830s and one of the most popular and widely read expositions of the siege story in the nineteenth century. It also demonstrated the fusion of sectarian politics with puritanical sexual and social values and the emotive, conversionist conception of religious experience that defined the impact of evangelical Protestantism both on Ulster society and the siege myth this period. Born the daughter of a Church of England clergyman in 1790, Elizabeth was both a committed ultra-Protestant proselytiser and a Tory. Although she visited Derry on only one occasion in 1838 (shortly after the publication of her novel) Elizabeth had taken a great interest in the activities of Protestant bible groups in Derry prior to this and was very closely involved the Reformation Society.

The theme of a feminised city standing out against attack thanks to spiritual help, communal sacrifice and moral virtue was signalled one of the most well-known songs of the siege myth, *The Maiden City* written by Elizabeth in the early 1830s. It was a view she developed in even greater depth in her novel. Elizabeth's story, of a virtuous Protestant family forced to flee to Derry and suffer the privations of the siege before ultimately being 'saved' by the relief of the city, illustrates how the cultural narrative of the siege could serve as a metaphor for the imagined life of the evangelical and provide a series of symbols through which an enthusiastic Protestant world-view could be established.

The Siege of Derry is both profoundly anti-Catholic and steeped in the ethos of conversion. Much of the book was designed to encourage the promotion of Protestantism among Irish Catholics through the Irish language. In real life this was a particular concern of Elizabeth's and her visit to Derry was a result of her links with the Londonderry Auxiliary to the Irish Society. This was hardly, however, a popular approach to the promotion of the 'Second Reformation' among Derry Protestants, as Elizabeth herself found on her visit to the city. Elizabeth may have viewed Irish Catholics as capable of 'reclamation' but she also saw them as a race of witless dupes, the simple victims of a pernicious and manipulative Catholic Church. In *The Siege of Derry* Catholics are portrayed as charming, loyal and emotional at best, the stuff of good servants; at worst they are barbaric, violent and deceitful, a portrait widely current in Victorian England that employed social Darwinism to explain Irish poverty and political unrest.[53] For Elizabeth the walls of Derry represented the line between the 'wild, fierce and restless' without, and those within. When she visited Derry Elizabeth described a brief trip she took to the Bogside in terms of a 'Christian soldier', advancing into enemy territory as she 'sallied through Butcher's Gate' to find the Bogside 'inhabited by an uncivilised population'.

1989, pp 4-9; Charlotte Elizabeth, *The siege of Derry: a tale of the revolution of 1688* (London, 1836). **53** L. P. Curtis, *Apes and angels: the Irishman in Victorian caricature* (Newton Abbot, 1971); R. N. Lebow, *White Britain and Black Ireland: the influence of stereotypes on colonial policy* (Philadelphia, 1985).

She looked forward to the day that she might regularly 'sally through that gate into the enemy's camp, after the fashion of 1689, armed with the sword of the spirit and seconded by a determined party of Irish Scripture readers'.[54]

Through the central heroine of her novel (Lady McAllister) Elizabeth projected an idealised image of the virtuous Protestant woman who (while strong of character) is ultimately and definitively, passive. The promise of salvation through 'pious resignation' provides the central meaning of the siege story for Elizabeth, and the siege is seen as a parallel for the inner life of the devout Protestant. As the siege builds toward the climax of the Relief, the main characters experience a heightened emotional state and an ecstatic religious vision. At the same time the imagery of the 'chaste' Lady McAllister and the Maiden city become totally interwoven. Ultimately the temporal victory of the siege relief is twinned by the longed for psycho-sexual and spiritual release for the heroine. Fulfilling the doctrine of grace by election, Lady McAllister is carried by her faithful native Irish servant toward the 'only goal that can be desired without guilt, death'; just as the boom is broken and the Relief ships enter the Lough.[55]

The actions depicted in this climatic scene were similar to the physical manifestations of revivalism and, as Peter Gibbon argues the prostrations and fits evident during the Revival of 1859 had clear psycho-sexual undertones. The Relief of the siege works, therefore, at a variety of levels, delivering both the inner psychological release to the heroine and the external religious and political victory to Protestantism. In the end the struggle of Derry is sublimated into the rich seam of biblical imagery based on the 'shining citadel' or the 'strong city'. Elizabeth's novel was published in numerous popular editions, and it found as wide a readership in England as in Ireland. The appeal of the novel to an evangelical audience lay in the historical subject matter, the emotional tone and the moral message of the book, all of which were quite typical of Methodist and other enthusiastic Protestant literature of the day. Elizabeth's work emphasises the power of the siege to provide a total symbolic system for the representation of an evangelical Protestant world view.

PROTESTANTISM BESIEGED?: THE SIEGE MYTH AND 'ALL PROTESTANT UNION', 1830-1860

Charlotte Elizabeth also found in the siege myth, and the image of the walled city, a metaphor of Protestant communal solidarity. 'Disunion among the people of God', she argued, 'is ever the precursor of judgement'.[56] For Elizabeth

54 *Londonderry Sentinel*, 13 Oct., 1838. **55** Charlotte Elizabeth, *Siege of Derry*, p. 71. **56** Ibid., p. 34.

the siege taught the lesson that all Protestants should sink their doctrinal differences and stress instead their common theological and social bonds. In this belief Elizabeth reflected the religio-political policy that crystallised the fusion of a distinctly Protestant political culture with fundamentalist Protestantism; the concept 'All-Protestant Union'.

The campaign for 'All-Protestant Union', heralded by the leading evangelical Presbyterian preacher Henry Cooke from the mid-1830s onward, gave the clearest expression of a Protestant collective identity in the early nineteenth century. Initially concerned with defending the privileges of the established church, and also at first a far from uncontested position amongst Ulster Presbyterians, All-Protestant Union emerged as a clarion call with far wider social and political repercussions. Diminishing the importance of inter-Protestant differences and emphasising the supposed common threat posed by Catholicism, All-Protestant Union became, in effect, the slogan of a new political consciousness. Significantly many of the leading advocates of Protestant Union were also strong supporters of the siege culture with its narrative of all-Protestant resistance. Here again, the siege myth was deeply affected by the times.

Not only did the rhetoric of the siege offer a series of symbols to establish inter-Protestant unity but the practices and organisations of the parades and the Apprentice Boys Clubs were means of combating the schismatic tendency of Ulster Protestantism. Unlike the Catholic community, where the single edifice of the Catholic Church helped to consolidate a sense of collective identity, Ulster Protestantism was structurally divided into two main churches, Episcopalian and Presbyterian, and accompanied by dozens of other sects and factions that multiplied in number during this period. As with the Orange Order, the Apprentice Boys Clubs acted as an organisational arena in which inter-Protestant cohesion could be established. That the leadership of the Apprentice Boys Clubs was dominated by members of the Church of Ireland but the membership was mostly Presbyterian emphasises the cohesive function the Clubs performed within the Derry Protestant community.

The campaign for All-Protestant Union was originally launched in support of the tithe privileges of the established church at the 'Hillsborough Demonstration' of 1834, described by Flann Campbell as the first occasion when 'extreme Toryism and Protestant fundamentalism first came together successfully in a mass meeting'.[57] This set in motion an increasing stress within Ulster politics upon the historical myth of the 'whole Protestant community'; the notion that Protestants shared (and had always shared) common interests,

---

57 Flann Campbell, *The dissenting voice: Protestant democracy in Ulster from plantation to partition* (Belfast, 1991) p. 161; R. G. F. Holmes, *Henry Cooke* (Belfast, 1981); R. M. Sibbert, *Orangeism in Ireland and throughout the Empire*, vol. 1 (London, 1939).

beliefs and traditions. It was an idea that would prove one most powerful ideological forces in late nineteenth-century Irish society.

Cooke's position was certainly hotly contested within the Presbyterian ministry in the mid-1830s and the Derry-based Moderator of the Ulster Synod,
William McClure, was a sometime critic of Cooke who sought to emphasise the
theological distinctiveness of Presbyterianism. Significantly too an anti-estab-
lishment element was evident within Derry Presbyterianism that would continue to be a significant political force through to the 1850s and 1860s. Based
largely on the interests and support of Presbyterian tenant farmers in countryside and local industrialists and businessmen in the city, liberal
Presbyterianism laid claim to a libertarian tradition that accentuated (rather
than ignored) the social, political and theological differences between
Presbyterians and the Church of Ireland. Derry had a narrow inter-Protestant
denominational balance so any political movement that tended to stress
Protestant denominational differences was liable to have a very significant
political impact.

The leading figure of Derry liberal Presbyterianism was James McKnight,
who became editor of the *Londonderry Standard* in 1848. A fierce critic of the
Established Church and of landlordism, McKnight was a leading activist of
the tenants rights agitation and the driving force behind attempts to establish
a distinct Presbyterian political structure within Derry during the 1850s. The
Standard had been established 1836 and soon emerged, alongside the *Northern
Whig* as the main voice of liberal opinion in Ulster. On numerous occasions the
Standard evoked a libertarian version of the siege myth as a means to histori-
cise its political message. Indeed the banner head of the paper featured a picture of Walker's Pillar emblazoned with the legend 'Our Faith and Our
Firesides'. Nor did the *Standard* report marches through the 1840s and 1850s
in anything other than glowing terms. Indeed, the owner of the *Standard* from
the 1840s onward was William Glendenning who was also one of the major figures active within the Apprentice Boys movement and the main organiser of
the Murray Club founded in 1847. Significantly, by the 1860s this liberal
Presbyterian lobby would call for the ending of the parades as they were seen
to be increasingly identified with 'High Tory, No Popery' sentiment.[58]

Indeed, members of both major denominations were involved in the
Apprentice Boys, although a degree of separation was apparent within the
movement. The members of Walker and Murray clubs founded in the 1840s
appear to have been mostly Anglicans and Dissenters respectively. Nor was it
inevitable that the doctrine of All-Protestant Union, which certainly later
dominated the outlook of the Apprentice Boys, would inevitably do so. However,
a growing stress on a rapprochement between Presbyterian and Episcopalian is

58 Cecil D. Milligan, *Centenary of the Murray Club*, p. 3.

apparent within the Apprentice Boys in this period. That rapprochement was instigated by fundamentalist and conservative Presbyterians.

Inter-Protestant rapprochement was signalled in a number of ways in which the siege parades were organised during the 1840s and 1850s. For example, the practice of holding of separate siege services in the Cathedral and the Presbyterian meeting house (that was the norm in the early 1840s) was replaced by a rule introduced by a newly formed general committee of the various clubs that the December service be held in the former and the August service in the latter.[59]

However, it was in the imagery of the siege as an imagined metaphor for All-Protestant solidarity that the siege myth played its most important role. In 1858, for example, when Henry Cooke's close ally and confidante, George Steen gave the siege address he not only extolled the virtues of temperance and the need for a religious revival but also cast this message in terms of the need for unity amongst all Protestants. 'Oh for a band of warriors like the immortal Walker,' Steen declared, who would 'fight under one banner, and struggle together to obtain the stainless robe of Christ without a rent or trace of superstition ... the hour is not far distant when all denominations of Christians shall unite to carry out that glorious truth of Protestantism'.[60]

It was significant that Steen should use Walker to drive this message home. The Walker cult had grown increasingly through the 1830s and 1840s. Several editions of his diary were published, a number of memorials had been erected to him and Walker's Pillar had become a major focal point for the siege practices, particularly after 1842 when it became the annual site for the burning of Lundy's effigy. That Walker should be celebrated as a model by a Presbyterian minister was far from natural. Walker had in fact symbolised for Presbyterians of previous generations the inequities they had suffered in the aftermath of the siege. His account had been fiercely contested by numerous Presbyterian and his disparaging remarks about the role of Presbyterians had been the subject for expressing Protestant diversity, not unity. But by the late 1850s fundamentalist advocates of All-Protestant Union, who opposed the liberal Presbyterian lobby, regularly invoked the image of Walker as the paragon of Protestant value.

Walker had also emerged as an archetype of an increasingly prominent element within Protestant politics, the politically active popular cleric, the 'pastor-politician', the 'warrior-priest'. The enthusiastic Protestant leader was one of the most powerful political figures of the late nineteenth century and Walker became the historical and cultural icon legitimating their message of aggressive Protestantism and direct political action. Writing just a few years

59 Colby, Col. R. E., *Ordnance Survey*, p. 182; Cecil D. Milligan, *Centenary of the Murray Club*; Centenary *of the Walker Club*. 60 *Derry Standard*, 17 Aug. 1858.

after Steen, Hugh Hanna (perhaps the most famous of these pastor-politicians) spoke on the subject of the Derry siege. It was a story, Hanna declared, that showed the Apprentice Boys had been 'loyal to the Crown and the Constitution' and in scenes 'consecrated by our fathers blood' they had defended their 'high moral virtues as 'united churchmen and Presbyterians'. The message of the siege for Hanna was simple, 'Protestant Union, the more effectually to resist the aggression of the Papacy, was the moral of it'.[61]

CONCLUSION: PROTESTANTISM, MODERNITY AND THE SIEGE MYTH

Hanna's words were a perfect reflection of what the siege myth had come to represent by the mid-nineteenth century. That was reflected, too, in how the siege culture was now organised and practised. Although the local aristocracy had long since ceased to take an active part in the siege parades, the corporation and the local political elite still favoured it with their patronage. Defence of the Protestant constitution was metamorphosing into the support of the Union and the siege had become identified with the moral values of mid-Victorian bourgeois society and the imagination of evangelical Protestantism. The Apprentice Boys clubs, not yet the vehicles of mass political mobilisation they were to become, were, nevertheless, increasingly routinised in their activities and consciously promoting inter-Protestant solidarity. All-Protestant Union represented a synthesis of politicised Protestantism and the influence of evangelicalism and had a decisive influence of the siege culture. The imagery of the siege myth had become a means to root, historically, the key conception of Protestant solidarity in the face of Catholic opposition. The rhetoric of the siege and the Apprentice boys clubs founded in this period provided both the symbolism and the material institutional framework for constructing and ritually living out living inter-Protestant unity.

The character of Protestant evangelicalism in early nineteenth century Ireland, and the role of All-Protestant Union as a politico-religious policy, each reflect a key element of religions ideological role in society. While there is an obvious danger in attempting to reduce the complexity of religion and its social functions to short and simple prescriptions, it is possible to suggest a framework for analysing the role Protestantism played in the siege myth during the early nineteenth century. Anthony Giddens has argued that religion has two primary ideological functions, 'the transmuted representation of values which

---

61 Revd Hugh Hanna, *Weighed and waiting: an examination by the Rev. Hugh Hanna of a review by Revd A. Robinson of a lecture on the siege of Derry, by the Rev. Hugh Hanna* (Belfast, 1871), p. 13.

are in fact created by man in society and the provision of principled support
for an existing social and political order'.[62]

If religious belief systems can serve to legitimate power relations and define
social values they will necessarily do so by taking on specific forms at a particular time and in a particular place. The variation of such forms will operate
within certain parameters set, in part, by the overarching tradition within
which they occur, in this instance the text-orientated, salvationary strand of
Reformation Protestantism. However, the rapid social change initiated by the
onset of modernity and the rise of capitalist social relations during the nineteenth century also conditioned the form of the 'sacred' and the social values
which it incorporated. The emergence of this process in Ireland gave rise to a
particular pattern of religious norms and practices through which both individuals and collectives could comprehend their experience. For Derry
Protestants in particular the cultural representation of those values was partly
performed though the siege myth. As a result, by the 1850s the siege was in
every way a Protestant Myth in an increasingly Catholic city.

62 Anthony Giddens, *Capitalism and modern social theory: an analysis of the writings of Marx,
Durkheim and Max Weber* (Cambridge, 1971), p. 205.

Remembering the siege of Derry: the rise of a popular religious and political tradition, 1689-1989

Brian Walker

Commemoration of the siege of Derry, 1688-9, is an important annual concern for many Protestant and Unionist people today in Northern Ireland. Well-attended parades, church services and other ceremonies are held in Derry on two special dates every year. On or near 12 August the relief of the city at the end of the siege is recalled while on or near 18 December the closing of the city gates at the beginning of the siege is remembered. These acts of commemoration are attended not just by citizens of the city but by people from many parts of Northern Ireland. Supporters come from County Donegal as well as from Canada and Great Britain. In recent years there has been controversy and conflict over the parades in Derry and also over the parades of supporters in Belfast and Dunloy, County Antrim, on their way to Derry. This article will explore these commemorative events and will seek to explain why and when they have come to play such an important part in the annual religious and political calendar of Northern Ireland. Special attention will be paid to the role of the organisation of Apprentice Boys of Derry in the demonstrations.

Many commentators have remarked on the significance of the siege of Derry and these annual commemorations for the Protestant and Unionist community. It has been claimed that 'ever since' 1689 there has been significant celebration of the event in a manner similar to that experienced today.[1] Jonathan Bardon, in his history of Ulster, has written: 'For the Protestants of Ulster this epic defence gave inspiration for more than three centuries to come.'[2] In a reference to various dates in the Protestant historical calendar, such as the rebellion of 1641 and the battle of the Boyne of 1690, the social anthropologist, Dr Anthony Buckley, has commented: 'Of all these historical events, the siege has the greatest symbolic significance.'[3] In his book *Despatches from Belfast*,

1 For example, Aiken McClelland, *William Johnston of Ballykilbeg* (Lurgan, 1990), p. 69. 2 Jonathan Bardon, *History of Ulster* (Belfast, 1992), p. 158. 3 Anthony Buckley, 'Uses of history among Ulster Protestants' in Gerald Dawe and J.W. Foster (eds), *The poet's place: Ulster literature and society* (Belfast, 1991), p. 262.

journalist David McKittrick has remarked about the siege: 'In three centuries it has never lost its potency and immediacy as a symbol for unionists, for they believe that the enemy is forever at the gate, waiting for the sentry to fall asleep.'[4] Derry historian Brian Lacey in *Siege city: the story of Derry and Londonderry* has described how 'particularly since the early nineteenth century, the siege of Derry has provided a parable and a vocabulary for describing the Ulster Protestant condition'.[5]

From these comments and the evidence of the ongoing annual parades in Derry, it is clear that the siege and its commemoration play a vital part in contemporary Northern Ireland. Questions remain, however, about these popular celebrations. Has the siege always been remembered in the way that it is today and have these celebrations always enjoyed such wide support? What do we know about the origins of traditions associated with the commemoration of the siege, such as the burning of an effigy of the traitor, Lundy? The clubs of the Apprentice Boys of Derry are responsible now for running the annual events but it will be valuable to know how long they have performed this role? How has support grown for the Apprentice Boys since their formation? Why do the celebrations remain important today for large numbers of the population of Northern Ireland? This paper will seek to answer these questions. The subject of the reaction from Catholic and nationalist quarters to the commemorations will not be investigated here: as regards the nineteenth century this matter is well covered in Tom Fraser's article on the Derry celebrations.[6]

The role of the siege in Protestant culture from the late seventeenth to the twentieth centuries has been the subject of a number of modern studies. Sam Burnside has looked at how the siege has been celebrated in drama, verse and prose.[7] Ian McBride has examined early efforts to commemorate the siege and has analysed tensions within the Protestant community over this matter.[8] He has shown how divisions existed between Presbyterians and members of the Church of Ireland until the 1880s when he believes that a broad Protestant consensus emerged and the annual commemorations in Derry began to draw on increasing support throughout Ulster, thanks to the efforts of the Clubs of the Apprentice boys of Derry. This present study will concentrate on growth of support for the commemorations from the 1880s, although attention will also focus on the earlier period in order to highlight the great changes of the later period. McBride's book spends little time on developments after the 1880s and there is no detailed study of the growth of these commemorations

4 David McKittrick, *Despatches from Belfast* (Belfast, 1989), p. 29.   5 Brian Lacey, *Siege City: the story of Derry and Londonderry* (Belfast, 1990), p. 137.   6 T.G. Fraser, 'The siege: its history and legacy, 1688-1889' in M.G.R. O'Brien (ed.), *Derry/Londonderry: history and society* (Dublin, 1998).   7 Sam Burnside, ' "No temporising with the foe": literary materials relating to the siege and relief of Derry' in *Linen Hall Review* 5/3 (Autumn, 1988), pp 4-9.   8 Ian McBride, *The siege of Derry in Ulster Protestant mythology* (Dublin, 1997).

in the last one hundred years, apart from some useful studies of a number of the Apprentice Boys of Derry Clubs, written by Derry local historian, C.D. Milligan, in the decade 1945-55.[9]

I

For most of the first 100 years after the siege, it seems that public commemoration of events, 1688-9, was spasmodic and without wide support. The earliest, reliable, evidence of celebration of the siege in the eighteenth century is an entry in the diary of Dr William Nicolson, bishop of Derry, 1718-27, written on 1 August 1718, the anniversary (under the old calendar) of the ending of the siege: 'I read prayers (first and second services) at Londonderry: Col. Michelburne's bloody flag being hoisted the first time, on the steeple. Evening, splendid treat in the tholsel, fireworks and illuminations.'[10] Over the next half century, there are few references to the event: sources are limited due to the absence of a Derry newspaper until the 1770s. There is no evidence of popular commemoration of the siege, but there are records of occasional services or dinners in honour of the event.[11] This lack of support for commemoration of the siege is probably due in part to bitter Presbyterian/Anglican conflict which emerged locally immediately after the siege and which was heightened by early eighteenth-century legislation against Presbyterians, such as the Test Act of 1704 which banned them from the corporation until 1780.[12] By the last decades of the century such intra-Protestant rivalry had eased but not ceased.

Reports in the local press in the 1770s confirm that there had been some earlier celebrations of the siege but also that these had lapsed and were only renewed at this stage. In August 1772 the *Londonderry Journal* carried a resolution from a local guild which declared gratitude to the city's mayor because he had 'revived' the 'ancient custom of commemorating the equally glorious and memorable deliverance of this city . . .'[13] The newspaper describes the scene in Derry on the 1st of August, when the bells were rung, the flag was displayed on the cathedral steeple and the mayor, corporation and freemen processed to a service at the cathedral, followed later by a dinner and other

9 C.D. Milligan, *The Walker Club centenary, 1844-1944, with an historical record of the Apprentice Boys and biographical notes on Governor Walker* (Derry, 1944); *The Murray Club centenary 1847-1947: a hundred years of history of the Murray Club of Apprentice Boys of Derry, with the story of Murray's part in the defence of Derry in 1689* (Derry, 1947); *Browning memorials (with a short historical note on the rise and progress of the Apprentice Boys of Derry Clubs)* (Derry, 1952); *The centenary of the revival of the Mitchelburne Club, 1854-1954* (Derry, 1954). For their assistance in obtaining copies of these publications I am grateful to Mr Billy Coulter and Mr Tony Crowe. 10 Quoted in John Hempton (ed.), *Siege and history of Londonderry* (Derry, 1861), p. 41. 11 See McBride, *Siege of Derry in mythology*, p. 36. 12 Ibid., pp 24-7. 13 Hempton, *Siege*, pp 415-7.

festivities. The mayor declined to assemble the citizens for the August commemoration in 1773; thereafter this event was marked annually. Until 1775, the
anniversary of the shutting of the gates was a matter of 'private conviviality'
but from this date it became a public event: in December 1788 an effigy of the
traitor Lundy was burned for the first time.[14] By the 1770s there is evidence of
the involvement of clubs or societies of local citizens, which can be seen as
forerunners of the nineteenth-century Apprentice Boys clubs, although in the
late eighteenth century they usually met privately to celebrate the siege, were
often short-lived and played a minor role in the celebrations, organised nor-
mally by the corporation. From the mid-1770s units of local volunteer corps
and the city garrison joined the commemorations.

In 1788 and 1789 there were important centenary anniversary commemorations.[15] In early December 1788 the closing of the gates was remembered by
special church services in both the cathedral and a Presbyterian church, followed by a civic procession, a military parade and the burning of Lundy. It also
involved a special dinner, attended by town dignitaries as well as Catholic
clergy. In August 1789 commemoration of the breaking of the boom and the
relief of the city included a sizeable procession to the cathedral which involved
not only the members of the corporation but the Catholic bishop and his
clergy, as well as the Presbyterian clergy and elders. On both these occasions
the siege was commemorated as a great blow against tyranny which brought
liberty to people of all Christian denominations. At the service in the cathedral
in August the preacher, the Revd George Vaughan Sampson, urged that the
message from the example of their forefathers was not just 'Glory be to God
in the highest' but also 'on earth, peace, goodwill towards men'.[16] In the atmosphere of late eighteenth-century Ireland, with the rise of a tolerant Irish patri-
otism, events of 1688-9 were seen as part of the Glorious Revolution with its
constitutional benefits for all, embracing Presbyterians and members of the
Church of Ireland, and Protestants and Catholics.[17]

II

The next half century witnessed significant changes in how the siege was
commemorated in Derry. The closing of the gates in December became a more
popular event to be celebrated than the ending of the siege in August. Military
units from the city garrison played a part in the celebrations until the 1820s,
when their participation ended, due to government policy not to be involved in
events which were seen as partisan: locally raised units of volunteers, such as

14 Milligan, *Browning memorials*, p. 9.   15 Hempton, *Siege*, pp 77-88.   16 Lacey, *Siege city*, pp
154-8.   17 McBride, *Siege of Derry in mythology*, p. 14.

yeomanry, continued to parade on these occasions until the 1830s.[18] A monument, consisting of a column and statue, in honour of the siege governor, the Revd George Walker, was erected in the late 1820s. There is some evidence of Catholic involvement in the celebrations in the early years of the nineteenth century but this had stopped by the 1830s.[19] Reflecting the rise of Protestant/ Catholic tension in Ireland in the early nineteenth century, the siege came to be seen increasingly as a Protestant symbol.[20] Some Protestants, such as the editor of the *Londonderry Standard* (founded in 1832), continued to view the siege as a victory of liberty for all, but the commemorations in Derry by the 1830s were dominated by those who regarded the siege solely as a Protestant victory.

By the 1830s the civic authorities were no longer involved (except on special occasions) in the annual commemorations which were now run by clubs of Apprentice Boys. The first nineteenth-century club of the Apprentice Boys of Derry (so named after the apprentice boys who shut the city gates in the face of the forces of James II in 1688) was formed in 1813. It was based, however, in Dublin and drew its support from well-off supporters of the Union who had an interest in Derry; while it survived until the early twentieth century it met privately in Dublin and had little or no influence in Derry.[21] In 1824 the No Surrender Club of Apprentice Boys was formed in Derry. The Ordnance Survey memoirs recorded in the early 1830s the existence of three such clubs in the city, but noted that they were losing influence and would 'doubtless become gradually extinct'.[22] In 1835 a new club with the broad name of the Apprentice Boys of Derry Club was founded in Derry. The first rule of the club declared the aim of celebrating the anniversary of the siege while the second stated that in the formation of the club, members were not 'actuated by factions or sectarian feeling, which we consider would be at variance with the cause of civil and religious liberty, the celebration of its establishment being the special purpose for which our society was instituted'.[23]

Celebrations of the 150th anniversary of the siege were markedly low key, compared with the centenary. In December 1838, the closing of the gates was marked only by the flying of flags, a salvo of guns, the burning of Lundy and a 'bottle and glass' party in the corporation hall, presided over by the sheriff. It was noted that no Catholics were present and most of the Protestants were of the 'humbler class'.[24] 'Bottle and glass parties' were a common feature of

---

18 Hempton, *Siege*, pp 436–48, McBride, *Siege of Derry in mythology*, p. 48. 19 Milligan, *Walker Club*, p. 20. 20 McBride, *Siege of Derry in mythology*, pp 46–52. 21 *Apprentice Boys of Derry, list of members, 1879* (Dublin, 1879). 22 *Ordnance survey of the county of Londonderry, vol. 1: city and north western liberties of Londonderry, parish of Templemore* (Dublin, 1837), p. 198. Published in 1837 this comment probably refers to the situation before the founding of the Apprentice Boys of Derry Club in 1835. 23 *Report of the commissioners of inquiry, 1869, into the riots and disturbances in the city of Londonderry*, p. 207. Rules and byelaws of the Apprentice Boys of Derry Club, formed 1835. 24 *Londonderry Sentinel*, 22 Dec. 1838.

celebrations in this period and involved participants bringing their own alcohol: they were replaced by more respectable tea-drinking parties and soirées in the 1840s.[25] None of the Derry papers gave much coverage to the August celebrations in 1839, which involved a short march of some Apprentice Boys together with supporters from Enniskillen, and which seems to have been poorly supported.[26] The Belfast press carried no reports at all of the occasion.

The following fifty years saw the transformation of the popularity of these commemorations and of the fortunes of the Apprentice Boys. A number of new clubs were formed and these proved to be longer lasting and better organised than their predecessors. While the No Surrender Club and the Apprentice Boys of Derry Club were the only Derry-based clubs to survive from the pre-1839 period, new clubs formed in honour of heroes of the siege were the Walker Club (1844), the Murray Club (1847), the Mitchelburne Club (1845, revived 1854) and the Browning Club (1854, revived 1876).[27] The growth of the clubs in the 1840s and 1850s probably reflects the local scene where a rise in the number of Catholic inhabitants meant that by the 1850s Protestants were no longer a majority in the city.[28] Around 1859 a general committee was established to co-ordinate the clubs and the celebrations. The post of governor, as head of the committee and the clubs, was created in 1867 although it lapsed in 1871 and was then restored in 1876. The clubs were Derry-based and before the late 1880s it seems that most members were born or lived in Derry.[29] Club rules, as in the case of the Apprentice Boys of Derry Club did not exclude outsiders, but since membership required all members to attend club meetings once a month this made it difficult for people outside Derry to retain membership.[30]

By the late 1850s, commemorations in Derry were well-attended, a situation which reflected more than just a rise in local interest. As Aiken McClelland has pointed out, crucial to the rise in popularity for these events was the arrival of the railway in Derry.[31] The opening of the Derry/Coleraine line in 1852 and the Derry/Strabane line in 1854 meant that many more people could now attend the demonstrations. The Party Processions Act which banned political parades, 1850-71, did not prevent these commemorations because they were seen as civic rather than political events and the marchers avoided using political banners and party tunes, although there was conflict on a number of occasions in this period between Apprentice Boys and the authorities as well as Derry Catholic residents over some of the ceremonies connected with the anniversaries of the siege. The press in the late 1850s and 1860s recorded the

25 Milligan, *Walker club*, p. 40.   26 *Londonderry Sentinel*, 17 Aug. 1839.   27 McBride, *Siege of Derry in mythology*, p. 49; *Official tercentenary brochure*, pp 21-8.   28 McBride, *Siege of Derry in mythology*, p. 45.   29 *Report of commissioners, 1869*, pp 180, 195.   30 *Report of commissioners, 1869: rules of Apprentice Boys of Derry Club*, p. 207.   31 McClelland, *Johnston*, p. 71.

attendance at the celebrations of substantial numbers of visitors, both on-lookers and participants.[32] William Johnston, elected to parliament in 1868 as an independent Protestant Conservative candidate for Belfast, attended regularly from 1860.[33] By the 1870s the August celebrations had become more popular than those in December. By this period, while membership of clubs was restricted mainly to Derry residents, a category of honorary membership had grown up, in spite of opposition from at least one club.[34]

An important stage in the development of the organisation of Apprentice Boys clubs was the opening of a purpose built hall in Derry in 1877 for the use of all the clubs. The idea of such a centre was first floated in the late 1860s, the foundation stone was laid in 1873 and five years later a hall, in memory of the original Apprentice Boys of the siege, was opened. Costing £3,250, the new Apprentice Boys' Memorial Hall provided a meeting place for all the clubs, a room for initiation services into the movement and an assembly hall for speeches after 12 August church service. A contemporary newspaper account described the new hall as 'in the style prevalent in the fortified and baronial residences of Scotland and this northern province in the sixteenth and seventeenth centuries, chosen as being most suitable to its memorial character, and the events with which it is associated'.[35] In 1877 the general committee of the associated clubs adopted a common form of initiation service for all new club members.[36] The order of precedence of the clubs in the annual parades was decided by the 1880s, after considerable debate. A march of clubs around the walls and the firing of cannon, along with the cathedral service, were regular features of the 12 August commemorations. In 1888-9 the bicentenary of the siege was marked by extensive celebrations which involved not only the Apprentice Boys but also the corporation. The usual commemoration ceremonies were well attended and other features of the event in August included a mock breaking of the boom, in repeat of this action 200 years earlier. These occurrences involved both Apprentice Boys clubs and many visitors.[37]

While most of the customs and practices associated with the siege commemorations, which are evident in the twentieth century, were in place by this stage, it must be stressed that the extent of popular involvement was still limited. Evidence given in 1869 to an enquiry about riots in Derry revealed that total membership of all six Apprentice Boys clubs in that year stood at only around 300 ordinary members and 200 honorary members, while a letter of 1867 from J.C. Ferguson, Governor of the Apprentice Boys Clubs, appealing for funds for the new hall, referred to '300 active members'[38]. A newspaper

32 *Northern Whig*, 13 Aug. 1867.   33 McClelland, *Johnston*, p. 71.   34 F.J. Porter, *Be in earnest: a sermon delivered by the Revd F.J. Porter before the Mitchellburn Club on 12 Aug. 1863* (Derry, 1863), p. 21; *Report of commissioners*, 1869, p. 180.   35 *Belfast Newsletter*, 14 Aug. 1877. 36 Milligan, *Murray Club*, p. 5.   37 *Londonderry Sentinel*, 13 Aug. 1877.   38 *Report of commissioners, 1869*, pp 180 and 195. A letter from J.G. Ferguson, governor of the Apprentice

account in the *Northern Whig* 13 August 1870, described the August parade as totalling about 1,000, including 200 Apprentice boys and 4 bands. Numbers had probably grown by the bicentenary but since full membership was still confined largely to Derry residents it is unlikely that the total of Apprentice Boys had increased significantly. Considerable numbers of people from the surrounding countryside and further afield did come to view or even to join the parade but they were not involved formally. Attempts were made in the 1870s to establish clubs outside the city but these met with rejection from the general committee of the Apprentice Boys: 'no charter will be granted for use outside the city of Londonderry'.[39] By 1889, however, the important decision had been taken to allow the establishment of external local clubs, although at the bicentenary celebrations it seems that only a small number of such clubs was in existence.[40]

As regards the composition of the Apprentice Boys' clubs in this period, we may note the comment of the *Londonderry Sentinel* editorial about the August 1889 bicentenary celebration that it was 'emphatically a people's commemoration' with few 'prominent leaders'.[41] William Johnston MP was one of the few Unionist leaders involved regularly in these annual events in Derry.[42] The government enquiry of the late 1860s had revealed that the Apprentice Boys' clubs were made up mainly of 'respectable tradesmen', were generally supportive of the conservative party in Derry and included both Presbyterians and members of the Church of Ireland.[43] Efforts in the 1860s to alternate the August anniversary service between the Church of Ireland cathedral and a Presbyterian church foundered when First Derry Presbyterian church refused to allow the clubs to bring their banners into the church: after this the cathedral was the main site for these services.[44] Many middle class Derry Presbyterians supported the liberal party in the late 1860s and although this party collapsed in Derry in the early 1870s there is little evidence of their active involvement in the commemorations. Liberalism remained strong among rural Presbyterians in County Londonderry and elsewhere in Ulster until the 1885-6 general elections when most former liberals and conservatives joined a new Unionist movement.[45] Nonetheless, even in the late 1880s there is no sign of new, mass Presbyterian involvement in the siege celebrations or the Apprentice Boys clubs. The main Presbyterian liberal paper in Ulster, the *Northern Whig*,

Boys, 7 Dec. 1867, appealing for funds for the new hall described '300 active members'. David Miller, *Still under siege* (Lurgan, 1989), p. 70: report on 1870 parade from *Northern Whig*, 13 Aug. 1870. **39** *Official tercentenary brochure*, p. 36. **40** *Londonderry Sentinel*, 13 Aug. 1889. **41** Ibid. **42** McClelland, *Johnston*, p. 71. **43** *Report of commissioners, 1869*, pp 192 and 195. **44** J.S. Crawford, *Alleluia: the commemoration service, preached on 12 Aug. 1864, the 175th anniversary of the relief of Londonderry*, in the Strand Road Presbyterian Church (Derry, 1864). **45** See B.M. Walker, *Ulster politics: the formative years, 1868-86* (Belfast, 1989).

gave the August 1889 bicentenary events a mere six inches of column space, in contrast to the extensive coverage in the *Belfast Newsletter*.[46]

Commemoration of the siege in places outside Derry and by organisations other than Apprentice Boys Clubs should be considered. A survey of the contemporary press does reveal some celebration of the event in a range of places in Ulster in the half century between the 250th anniversary and the bicentenary in 1889. We read of instances such as an Orange dinner in Belfast on 18 December 1855 to mark the relief of the city (*sic*), an Orange demonstration near Lurgan on 12 August 1873 to celebrate the siege and the burning of effigies of Lundy in Larne on 18 December 1886.[47] Sometimes the 12th of August was used as the occasion for special Orange events such as the opening of an Orange hall, as in Portadown in 1875.[48] During these years, however, the celebrations were neither commonplace, widely supported nor organised annually. The major exception was in County Fermanagh where on 12 August, from the 1840s, the siege of Derry was commemorated frequently along with the battle of Newtownbutler (anniversary also 12 August) and other Fermanagh events of the 1688-9 wars.[49] At the bicentenary of the siege on 12 August 1889 there were major Orange celebrations only in Fintona, County Tyrone, and Kesh, County Fermanagh.[50] The attendance at Kesh was described as large, with a special train bringing brethren from Counties Tyrone and Donegal as well as County Fermanagh, but numbers were much lower than in Derry. One of the speakers at Kesh declared that 'They were descendants of the men who stood upon Derry's walls and who fought at the battles of Newtownbutler and Lisnaskea, and who manned the banks of the Erne. The descendants of these men would never let themselves be trampled upon.'[51]

Clearly then, the half century 1839-89 witnessed important change in the popularity of the siege celebrations and in the role and membership of the Apprentice Boys clubs. Demographic factors in Derry probably added this development while the improvement of transport facilities was a significant economic element which helped to open up the event to supporters from a much wider field than would have been possible before. The fact that Orange marches were banned during the 1850s and 1860s, while siege commemoration parades were allowed in Derry, may help to explain the rise in popularity of the latter. The continued growth in support for the celebrations in the 1870s and 1880s reflected undoubtedly the rise in political excitement and the emergence of unionist/nationalist confrontation throughout Ireland in this period. All this helped to give a new relevance to the story of the siege, especially to Derry Protestants. But until the late 1880s these annual commemorations had an

---

46 *Northern Whig*, 13 Aug. 1889.   **47** *Belfast Newsletter*, 20 Dec. 1855; *Belfast Telegraph*, 13 Aug. 1873; *Northern Whig*, 20 Dec. 1886.   **48** *Belfast Newsletter*, 13 Aug. 1875.   **49** *Impartial Reporter*, 14 Aug. 1845; *Londonderry Sentinel*, 17 Aug. 1849; *Impartial Reporter*, 15 Aug. 1872; 14 Aug. 1879; 16 Aug. 1888.   **50** *Belfast Newsletter*, 13 Aug. 1889; 14 Aug. 1889.   **51** Ibid., 14 Aug. 1889.

appeal to only a limited number of people, as reflected in the small extent of
siege celebrations outside Derry (even in 1889), the relatively low number of
outside participants at the Derry events and, particularly, the limited membership of the Apprentice Boys clubs. The decision of the general committee of
the Apprentice Boys in the late 1880s to allow the setting up of local branches
of the clubs was a momentous one. It meant that whereas the Derry siege had
become a special symbol for many Protestant residents of Derry, it could now
become one for others elsewhere. Why the decision to allow this was taken at
this stage is not clear. Perhaps, because of the emergence of strong national
parties and the major issue of home rule, Derry unionists now saw themselves
as part of the broader scene and members of the larger unionist and Protestant
community. This decision would have major consequences for the level of
broader involvement in the siege celebrations.

III

The half century after the bicentenary celebrations witnessed a dramatic
growth in the amount of popular support for the commemorations in Derry
and the Apprentice Boys' clubs. The key to this change was the decision, taken
in the 1880s, to allow the Derry-based clubs (now known as parent clubs) to
establish branch clubs outside the city. All members continued to be initiated
within Derry's walls. No annual returns are available for the total membership
of the Apprentice Boys' clubs but a good idea of the growth of the movement
can be gained from newspaper accounts of the number of clubs and the figures
of annual initiation. For the period 1889-1939 it is usually possible to obtain
from newspapers accurate information on the names and numbers of the clubs.
Annual figures for total numbers initiated are difficult to find in the early
period 1889-1923, because members of the various clubs were initiated at different times of the year, but from 1923 there were usually combined initiations
for all club members at the August commemorations and so reliable figures of
numbers initiated are often, but not always, available in the press post 1923.
Rarely in this period does the press record figures for the number on parade or
the total number present.

Initially, and perhaps surprisingly, the growth of these branch clubs was
slow. At the August 1889 celebrations, 3 branch clubs, all from Belfast, joined
the parade.[52] By August 1900 there were present at the August commemorations just 8 branch clubs (4 from Belfast, 2 from County Antrim, 1 from
County Armagh and 1 from County Down), although this meant that there
were now more branch than parent clubs (7 in 1900).[53] Celebrations in August

52 *Londonderry Sentinel*, 13 Aug. 1889.   53 Ibid., 14 Aug. 1900.

1914 for the 225th anniversary of the siege saw a low turn-out because of transport restrictions due to the war situation in Europe.[54] Two years earlier, however, the August parade included 17 branch clubs, of which there were 6 from Belfast, 3 County Antrim, 1 County Armagh, 5 County Down and 2 County Londonderry.[55] Clubs received a charter when no less than 13 members had been admitted to full membership of the Apprentice Boys; initiation had to occur within Derry's walls. In this period the December celebrations were confined to parent clubs.[56] Records for the clubs in the period 1900-14 show that a small number of branch clubs was established in Canada and Scotland.[57] From 1911 the general committee of Apprentice Boys clubs was allowed to nominate six members to the Ulster Unionist Council.[58] During the war the annual commemorations continued, although in a reduced form.

In 1920 riots in Derry led to all parades being banned but the usual church services were attended by members of the Apprentice Boys' clubs.[59] In 1923 a press report on the August parade recorded the presence of 17 branch clubs, a figure similar to club numbers present in 1912: upwards of 300 new members were initiated in August 1923.[60] From this time on, however, expansion in the number of clubs and initiations occurred rapidly. In 1924, for the first time, a Presbyterian minister preached in the cathedral at the August anniversary. The next day, the *Northern Whig*, unusually, devoted an editorial column to the celebrations, declaring that 'every loyalist in the province loves and claims a patriotic interest in the stones of Derry': this new degree of interest by the *Northern Whig* may be explained by the fear expressed in its editorial that under the threatened redrawing of the border Derry would be lost to the Free State.[61] Following the erection of a war memorial in the Diamond in the 1920s, the laying of wreaths by the leading party in the parade became an important feature of the commemorations. From the early 1920s new members were initiated at a joint ceremony usually held during the August commemorations. In 1927 the Baker Club was revived so that there were now 7 parent clubs. Branch club numbers on parade at the August commemorations increased to 31 in 1924, 51 in 1930 and 80 in 1936. In 1924 several hundred new members were initiated but by 1936 annual initiations totalled 800.[62] By 1939 the number of branch Clubs totalled 93 and 700 new members were initiated.[63]

Analysis of distribution of branches over this period reveals how the Apprentice Boys' organisation spread throughout Northern Ireland. In August 1923 the 17 branch clubs came from the following areas: Belfast 6, County Antrim 2, County Armagh 2, County Down 2, County Londonderry 3 and

54 *Belfast Newsletter*, 13 Aug. 1914. **55** Ibid., 13 Aug. 1912. **56** *Londonderry Sentinel*, 19 Dec. 1912. **57** Milligan, *Murray*, pp 38-41. **58** *For God and Ulster: an alternative guide to the loyal orders* (Derry, 1997), p. 14. **59** *Official tercentenary brochure*, p. 4. **60** *Londonderry Sentinel*, 14 Aug. 1923. **61** *Northern Whig*, 13 Aug. 1924. **62** *Northern Whig*, 13 Aug. 1924, *Londonderry Sentinel*, 14 Aug. 1930, and 13 Aug. 1936. **63** *Londonderry Sentinel*, 15 Aug. 1939.

County Tyrone 2.[64] The 51 branch clubs on parade in August 1930 belonged
to Belfast 7, County Antrim 7, County Armagh 7, County Down 9, County
Londonderry 8, County Tyrone 11 and County Donegal 2.[65] By the 250th
anniversary parade in August 1939 the 93 branch clubs were to be found in
Belfast 7, County Antrim 16, County Armagh 10, County Down 18, County
Fermanagh 2, County Londonderry 13, County Tyrone 15, County Donegal
6, Scotland 4 and England 2.[66] The sudden growth in Donegal branches in this
decade is probably explained by the restrictions on Orange parades in Donegal
post 1932. The Scottish branches came from Govan, Partick, Springburn and
Glasgow while the English branches came from Liverpool and Birkenhead.
These figures relate to the number of branches on parade and so may underestimate slightly the total number of clubs in existence, as some, especially
from Canada and Scotland, may not always have attended.[67]

Although the number of clubs in Belfast during this period 1921-39
increased only by one after the founding of a Belfast branch of the newly
revived Baker Club, their membership grew rapidly. In 1925 a charter was granted
to create a Belfast and District Amalgamated Committee to co-ordinate the
Belfast branches.[68] In 1939 the Belfast branch of the Browning Club had 300
members on parade in Derry, the largest turn out of any club or branch.[69]
Plans were drawn up in this period to build a hall for the Belfast clubs, but this
never materialised and the clubs continued to avail of Orange halls, as did all
the other branch clubs.[70] A Mid-Ulster Amalgamated Committee was in existence by the early 1930s. By the mid 1930s the Apprentice Boys' organisation
was holding parades on Easter Monday in different centres around Northern
Ireland for parent and branch clubs.[71] In 1936 the foundation stone for a large
extension to the Apprentice Boys' Memorial Hall in Derry was laid by the
city's lord mayor, Captain J.M. Wilton.[72] Costing £30,000, the new premises
were opened in 1938 by Viscountess Craigavon to provide extensive additional
accommodation which included a large assembly hall to seat nearly 2,000 people, rooms for the meetings of clubs and local Orange and Black lodges, and
new social facilities. In this period we can note the initiation of some prominent politicians into the Apprentice Boys clubs, although apart from Derry
politicians, they seem to have played little regular part in the commemorations.
In 1933, for example, Dawson Bates, minister of home affairs in the Northern
Ireland government and Price, attorney general of Toronto, were initiated into
the Murray Club.[73]

64 *Londonderry Sentinel*, 14 Aug. 1923. 65 Ibid., 14 Aug. 1930. 66 Ibid., 15 Aug. 1939.
67 Ibid. 68 *Official tercentenary brochure*, p. 38. 69 *Londonderry Sentinel*, 15 Aug. 1939.
70 *Official tercentenary brochure*, p. 38. 71 Although the tercentenary brochure suggests that
Easter parades started in 1925, this is not confirmed by press reports. 72 *Londonderry Sentinel*,
13 Aug. 1936. 73 Milligan, *Murray Club*, p. 45.

Celebrations in Derry city in 1938-9 to mark the 250th anniversary of the siege were very extensive. The December 1938 commemoration of the closing of the gates was better attended than usual, with a special train bringing supporters from Belfast.[74] The main emphasis for the 250th anniversary came at the 12 August 1939 demonstrations for the anniversary of the relief of the city. The *Londonderry Sentinel* reported that 'all morning until noon, Apprentice Boys and their friends, who grow more numerous every year, poured into the city from every part of Northern Ireland and the border districts of Eire'.[75] A total of 21 ordinary and special trains, about 100 buses and many cars brought upwards of 20,000 people to the city. The huge procession consisted of 100 Apprentice Boy Clubs (both parent and branch Clubs) and around 100 bands. At the service in the cathedral, the preacher was Dr James Little, a Presbyterian minister and Unionist MP for North Down. His sermon was primarily a religious one but he referred to current threats from the southern government and militant republicans:

> To all who are seeking in one way or another to undermine our state we send today this message from the historic walls of Derry, that neither to politician nor terrorist will we ever consent to surrender any portion of the inheritance which God has entrusted to us.[76]

In its editorial the *Londonderry Sentinel* stressed the relevance of the siege in face of contemporary threats at home and abroad.[77]

An important feature of the half century following the bicentenary of the siege was the growth in celebration of the event in centres outside Derry on 12 August by organisations other than the Apprentice Boys. Whereas in August 1889 there were only important demonstrations in Kesh in County Fermanagh and in Fintona in County Tyrone, both organised by the Orange Order, by the early 1900s there were additional demonstrations in both counties and supporters from counties Donegal, Cavan, Londonderry, Armagh and Monaghan were involved, sometimes on their own and sometimes in joint demonstrations.[78] By 1910, however, organisation of these 12 August anniversary celebrations was almost entirely run by preceptories of the Royal Black Order, rather than the Orange Order, although Orange lodges sometimes attended the parades. In 1910 on 12 August there were demonstrations not only at a number of centres in Tyrone and Fermanagh, but also Annaghmore, County Armagh and Cavan, County Cavan.[79] During the 1920s and 1930s well attended demonstrations were held by the Royal Black Order on 12 August in

---

74 *Londonderry Sentinel*, 20 Dec. 1938. **75** Ibid., 15 Aug. 1939. **76** Ibid. **77** Ibid. **78** *Belfast Newsletter*, 13 and 14 Aug. 1889; 14 Aug. 1900. **79** *Belfast Newsletter*, 13 Aug. 1910, *Armagh Guardian*, 13 Aug. 1910.

different locations in south and mid Ulster.[80] Post 1932 such parades ceased in
counties Cavan, Monaghan and Donegal due to local republican opposition but
brethren from these counties attended parades in Northern Ireland.[81] At
the 250th anniversary of the siege on 12 August there were Black-run demonstrations in Cookstown, Drumquin, and Ballygawley, County Tyrone, and
Irvinestown, County Fermanagh. Those attending came from all the nine
Ulster counties, except Down and Antrim.[82]

The growth in support for the Apprentice Boys organisation and its celebrations in Derry, as well as parades elsewhere, clearly reflects the expanding
significance of the Derry story in the new political and religious confrontation
of post-1886 Ireland. The fact that the rise of such support was strongest after
1921 may be related to the new, exposed situation of Derry on the border of
Northern Ireland. It may also be the result of a general rise in interest in this
period in loyal orders, such as the Junior Orange Association, founded in
1925.[83] It has been argued that support for the Orange Order declined in the
period 1921–39, but it is possible that this was because individuals were joining
other organisations, such as the Apprentice Boys.[84] While membership of the
Apprentice Boys organisation was undoubtedly influenced by the political situation, the religious situation was also significant. By the 1920s the commemorations in Derry no longer included meetings for political speeches but
centred largely on the religious services held in the cathedral. Increased support for the Derry parades may be seen as evidence of a growth in popular
Protestantism, uniting different denominations, as well as a rise in political
unionist activity. Interesting comment on the new pervasiveness of the Derry
story can be found in the account of celebrations and anniversaries in the
history of Enniskillen, written by W.C. Trimble and published in 1921.[85] He
claimed that Orangemen in Enniskillen on 12 July and 12 August 'while they
celebrate the deeds of other places, ignore the resolve of their own townsmen
to close their East Bridge to King James' soldiers in December 1688 and to
their own great victory at Newtownbutler'. He hoped that his history would
help to cure 'this ignoring of the Enniskillen men by Enniskillen men.'

80 *Belfast Newsletter*, 13 Aug. 1923; *Northern Whig*, 13 Aug. 1930.   81 Aiken McClelland, 'The
Orange Order in Co. Monaghan' in *Clogher Record* (1978), p. 387.   82 *Belfast Newsletter*, 13 Aug.
1939. There are instances of Black preceptories from Down and Antrim attending these 12
August commemorations in South Ulster or in their own counties in the 1920s and 1930s but they
are few.   83 *Junior Orange Association of Ireland, Belfast County Lodge 1925-75* (Belfast, 1975).
84 David Fitzpatrick, *The two Irelands, 1912-39* (Oxford, 1998) p. 178.   85 W.C. Trimble, *The
history of Enniskillen: with references to some manors in Co. Fermanagh*, vol. 3 (Enniskillen, 1921),
pp 77-89.

IV

During the second world war the public celebrations of the siege in Derry were cancelled by the Apprentice Boys' general committee. In August 1946, at the first peacetime demonstration since the war, a record number of 2,500 to 'nearly 3,000' members were initiated at ceremonies which, according to the *Londonderry Sentinel*, 'continued from 9.00 a.m. till 5.00 p.m.'[86] The *Sentinel* also noted that 'over 10,000 free drinks were served by the Londonderry Temperance Council from thirteen specially erected stalls along the processional route'. In the same year it was reported that the procession contained 7,000 Apprentice Boys and 90 bands.[87] In 1947 the preacher at the August cathedral service, the Revd J.G. MacManaway, MP and Church of Ireland clergyman, declared:

> We in Ulster have our own Holy Place, our own religious shrine to which our history as Protestants forever joins us. The Protestant shrine of Protestant Ulster is forever Derry. We do not meet together to provoke anybody or criticise any man's faith. But, just as our forefathers before us, we are resolved that we shall not be driven out of this country by political pressure or economic measures to deprive us of our freedom and our faith.[88]

During the late 1940s and 1950s numbers of members initiated frequently reached or passed the 1,000 mark.[89] Press reports on the commemorations after the war no longer list the names of all the clubs taking part and only occasionally do they record their numbers. We may note, however, that in 1950 and 1958 it was reported that 120 branches were present at the August parades, along with a similar number of bands.[90] Actual numbers of Apprentice Boys in the parade varied between 5,000 and 8,000.[91] In light of the large number of annual initiations it seems clear that all members did not attend every year. It is difficult to give precise figures of those present but press estimates ranged between 30,000 and 40,000.[92] Attendances could be affected by whether or not demonstrations were held on a Saturday.

The number of parent Clubs increased to eight with the revival of the

86 Ibid., 13 Aug. 1946 (nearly 3000); *Northern Whig*, 13 Aug. 1946 (2500).   **87** *Northern Whig*, 13 Aug. 1946.   **88** *Belfast Newsletter*, 13 Aug. 1947.   **89** *Northern Whig*, 15 Aug. 1949; 13 Aug. 1951; 11 Aug. 1952; *Londonderry Sentinel*, 13 Aug. 1957; 13 Aug. 1958.   **90** *Londonderry Sentinel*, 15 Aug. 1957; 13 Aug. 1958.   **91** *Northern Whig*, 12 Aug. 1946 (over 7,000); ibid., 13 Aug. 1947 (6000); *Belfast Newsletter*, 13 Aug. 1957 (8,000); *Londonderry Sentinel*, 19 Aug. 1959 (5,000). On 13 Aug. 1946 the *Londonderry Sentinel* reported that over 12,000 Apprentice Boys attended the parade but this is probably exaggerated.   **92** *Londonderry Sentinel*, 15 Aug. 1950 (40,000); ibid., 13 Aug. 1953 (30,000).

Campsie Club in 1950. This period also saw the formation of a number of amalgamated committees for different areas: Scotland (1946), Ballymena and district (1948), South Down (later County Down) (1948), Coleraine and district (1948), South Derry and East Tyrone (1954). In 1963 an amalgamated committee for South West Ulster was formed to cover Monaghan, Cavan, South Donegal, Fermanagh and West Tyrone.[93] The general committee of Apprentice Boys was extended to include representatives from these committees. Until the 1950s the December parades were attended primarily by members of parent clubs with only a few representatives from other clubs but after this time more members from outside attended the commemoration of the closing of the gates, although numbers were still much lower than in August. In 1961 centenary celebrations for the founding of the Browning Club was the occasion for the first Methodist minister to preach in the cathedral.[94] During the 1960s the number of annual August initiations seems to have dropped to around 500 but at this time December initiations became more popular than before. The parades continued to attract large numbers of Apprentice Boys, bands and on-lookers. On 15 August 1962, the *Londonderry Sentinel* reported that:

> The parade was so long that it filled the entire two and a half miles long processional route from the Diamond, via Carlisle Road, the Bridge, Duke Street . . . The last contingents had not left the Diamond when the head of the procession had returned and was passing through the Diamond to the walls.

In Scotland Apprentice Boys Clubs celebrated only with church services until 1959 when the first open air rally was held at Caldercruix. Since then the Scottish amalgamated committee has organised its main rally on the 3rd Saturday in May.[95]

On the 275th anniversary of the siege in 1964, the number visiting the city on 12 of August was put at 35,000, a figure which was slightly down from the total of 40,000 two years earlier when the August commemoration fell on a Saturday.[96] Numbers of those initiated were recorded as around 500 in August 1962 and August 1964 (100 others were initiated in December 1964)[97]. In August 1964 it was reported that the two and a half mile long parade contained more than 100 clubs, 5,000 Apprentice Boys and 100 bands, and took one 1 hour and 10 minutes to pass Carlisle Square.[98] It was estimated that on the same occasion 19 Ulster Transport Authority trains, 160 Ulster Transport

93 *Official tercentenary brochure*, pp 37-42.   94 W.J. Wallace, *Browning Club Apprentice Boys of Derry* (Derry, 1961), p. 37.   95 *Official tercentenary brochure*, p. 37.   96 *Londonderry Sentinel*, 15 Aug. 1962; 19 Aug. 1964.   97 Ibid., 22 Dec. 1964.   98 Ibid., 19 Aug. 1964.

Authority buses and 3,000 cars were required to bring the visitors to the city. The Lough Swilly Company brought 500 visitors from County Donegal. The press reported that there were representatives from Canada, Scotland, Liverpool and Philadelphia, as well as contingents from Countys Donegal and Monaghan. By the 1960s the initiation of prominent politicians was common-place although few of them seem to have played a regular part in commemorations. Two prime ministers of Northern Ireland, Lord Brookeborough (1960) and Captain Terence O'Neill (1964), were initiated in this period. Brian Faulkner, minister of commerce, was initiated in 1966: that same year in the Ulster Unionist Council year book he welcomed the involvement of young people in politics, stating that 'going right back to the Apprentice Boys our young men and now young women too have been quick to sense the need for action and to give a lead'.[99]

Although it is difficult to give a complete picture of the strength of the Apprentice Boys movement in this period, because newspapers no longer record the names of branches, we are able to gain an important insight into the organisation's composition from an official Apprentice Boys' printed list of branch clubs, branch club secretaries and local place of meeting for the year 1971.[100] It records a grand total of 178 branches, but notes that in nine cases the branches made no return of information which implies that they were defunct. As regards these 178 branches their distribution was as follows: Belfast 16, County Antrim 31, County Armagh 16, County Down 28, County Fermanagh 5, County Londonderry 22, County Tyrone 35, County Donegal 7, Scotland 14, England 2, Canada 2 and USA 1. In comparison with the fig-ures for 1939, this record reveals a number of interesting developments, espe-cially the growth in the number of Scottish and Belfast branches. This 1971 list records eight amalgamated committees as well as a general committee of 12 officers and 33 members. Clearly this picture shows considerable growth, although to some extent, as in the case of Belfast, it may simply reflect the breakaway of clubs from existing clubs into new clubs rather than a real increase in the numbers of Apprentice Boys actually involved.

Since 1970 the form of the siege commemorations has changed consider-ably. After riots in the city in 1969 following the 12 August parade, a ban was imposed on Apprentice Boys parades during 1970 and 1971, although services continued in the cathedral. In the period 1972–5 the August procession was restricted to the Waterside. In 1975 the parade was allowed into the walled city during the August commemoration but it was confined to the upper part of the city and marches around the walls continued to be banned: only from 1995 have parent clubs been allowed to march around the city walls again. The

99 *Ulster Unionist Council Yearbook*, 1966 (Belfast, 1966). **100** *Apprentice Boys of Derry, member's ticket*, 1971 (Dungannon, 1971), (copy in the Linen Hall Library, Belfast).

burning of Lundy from Walker's monument was banned by government order in 1970 and the monument itself was blown up in 1973, but this did not end the December siege celebrations. Since 1970 the effigy of Lundy has been burned in nearby Bishop Street. The December parades were also banned during 1970-5, but have continued in a restricted form since then. In the mid-1970s the formal link between the Apprentice Boys general committee and the Ulster Unionist Council was broken with the ending of the nomination of six members to the Council. In 1984, a demonstration of Apprentice Boys was held in London to protest against the change of the name of the city from Londonderry to Derry. During these decades several new amalgamated committees were formed, including one for England.

It is not easy to assess numbers of clubs, Apprentice Boys on parade or new members initiated during the two decades 1969-89 because press reports are scanty in their information on these subjects: figures for initiations are also more difficult to find because during this period the ceremony was performed at various times, not just in December and August. As regards numbers of those initiated it seems that 1960s levels have been maintained, if we judge by figures for August 1979 (400) and August 1985 (600): in 1982 640 were initiated in August and 100 in December.[101] Figures for those present at the commemorations in August ranged from 5,000 in 1972 to 20,000 in 1985: the security situation undoubtedly effected these numbers.[102] Two of the few press references to the number of Apprentice Boys in the procession put them at 7,000 in 1977 and 10,000 in 1988, while several Apprentice Boys sources put full membership at 11,000-12,000 by 1988.[103] Numbers of bands increased during the period from 139 in 1977 to 160 in 1989.[104] There are no accounts in the press of the number of branches on parade during these decades but we do know that there were 178 in 1971 and, according to the official Apprentice Boys tercentenary brochure, over 200 by 1988.[105] Although this latter figure has been questioned there is evidence of the growth of new Clubs in these years. In August 1982, for example, there were new branches at the parade from Newmills (County Tyrone), Ballinakillen (County Donegal), Clough (County Down), Portrush (County Antrim) and Dalry (Scotland).[106] A special feature of this last period has been the increase in the number of branches in Scotland and England.

101 Ibid., 15 Aug. 1979; *Belfast Telegraph*, 13 Aug. 1985; *Londonderry Sentinel*, 18 Aug. and 22 Dec. 1982. 102 Ibid., 16 Aug. 1972; *Belfast Telegraph*, 12 Aug. 1985. 103 *Londonderry Sentinel*, 17 Aug. 1977; *Belfast Newsletter*, 15 Aug. 1988; General-Secretary Derek Miller put total membership at 11,000 in 1988, *Belfast Telegraph*, 15 Aug. 1988; a figure of 12,000 is given in the *Official tercentenary brochure*, p. 37. 104 *Londonderry Sentinel*, 17 Aug. 1977; 16 Aug. 1989; 15 Aug. 1988. 105 *Apprentice Boys of Derry, member's ticket 1971* (Dungannon, 1971), (copy in the Linen Hall Library, Belfast). 106 *Londonderry Sentinel*, 18 Aug. 1982.

The tercentenary of the siege was the occasion of extensive celebrations in the city. The Apprentice Boys' organisation co-operated with the nationalist city council in various functions and commemorative events. In August 1989 characters in period costume re-enacted scenes from the siege and a mock breaking of the boom was staged.[107] Local councils elsewhere, such as Omagh and Lisburn, organised civic receptions for representatives of the Apprentice Boys organisation. In May a parade of Apprentice Boys was held in Edinburgh to mark the tercentenary. At the cathedral service in Derry on 12 August 1989 the preacher, the Revd James Kane, spoke of the many deaths and destruction of the previous 20 years.[108] In an official Apprentice Boys tercentenary brochure, which referred to both the general political situation and the local reduction of the number of Protestants on the west bank of the city, the chairman of the tercentenary committee wrote: 'the siege of Derry is, in many senses, still going on'.[109] Other publications at this time included a book on the siege by Peter Robinson MP in which he declared: 'For three centuries Londonderry has been the symbol of Protestant resolve and dogged determination to stand against any threat to its inhabitants and their way of life.'[110]

Continued expansion of the Apprentice Boys' organisation in the half century 1939-89 can be explained by a number of factors. Clearly the siege of Derry continued to be a potent symbol for more and more Unionists and Protestants in Northern Ireland. For the first two decades of this period, however, a special factor was the shift in emphasis by the Royal Black Order in its August parades from 12 August to its other day of parades on the last Saturday of August. During the 1950s in all counties, except in Fermanagh, demonstrations on 12 August ceased outside Derry, thus freeing members of the Black Order, and Orange supporters, to join the Apprentice Boys' Clubs and to attend the Derry celebrations.[111] Sometimes Black preceptories would mark 12 August with church services but this date was no longer the occasion for major Black parades. Continuation of 12 August celebrations in County Fermanagh may be explained by a rise in local interest in the battle of Newtownbutler (also celebrated on 12 August) and other county Fermanagh events of 1688-9. Expansion in the number of clubs and members since 1969 should be seen as part of the growing interest in loyal orders and parades in the Unionist community as a result of the 'troubles' in Northern Ireland. Dr Neil Jarman has stated: 'In recent years, and perhaps particularly since the signing of the Anglo-Irish Agreement in 1985, Protestants have felt their constitutional position, and therefore their sense of national identity, more threatened than at any time since partition.' One response, he says, 'has been to parade more

107 Ibid., 16 Aug. 1989. **108** Ibid. **109** *Official tercentenary brochure*, p. 3. **110** Peter Robinson, *Their cry was 'No Surrender': an account of the siege of Londonderry, 1688-9* (Belfast, 1988), pp 17-18. **111** *Belfast Newsletter*.

frequently in local areas, and also to organise more parades for more events'.[112]
The rise in outside support for this particular event is perhaps attributable to
the symbolic loss of Derry to nationalist control and the reduction in the number of Protestants in Derry and a consequent felt need to show Protestant and
Unionist solidarity.

V

The siege of Derry is recalled today by many members of the Protestant and
Unionist community in Northern Ireland who annually celebrate the event in
well attended parades, church services and other ceremonies in Derry. It is
clear, however, that there has not always been such deep interest in the subject,
as various writers, quoted at the beginning of this article, have alleged. It is not
true that 'ever since' 1689 the event has been celebrated in a fashion similar to
that today: commemorations in Derry have evolved considerably over the last
three hundred years. We do not know how far memories of the siege remained
in the consciousness of Protestants, but evidence of their concern, as expressed
in their degree of support for these commemorations in Derry and elsewhere,
does not suggest that the siege has been either a major source of inspiration or
of great symbolic value ever since1688-9. From our knowledge of celebrations
of the siege in Derry, it is clear that there was a substantial period when there
was little popular commemorations of these historic events, there were times
when the siege was seen in an inclusive light, and, of course there were long
periods when the siege served as a great Protestant and Unionist symbol,
although the number of people involved in this last stage greatly altered in
time. The most marked growth in popular support for commemoration of the
siege was not in the early nineteenth century, nor indeed in the late nineteenth
century, but in the period post 1921. The extent of the marked change which
occurred in the popular appreciation of the siege can be seen in the contrast
between celebrations in August in Derry in 1839 and a century later in 1939.
On the former occasion small numbers of locals, with some visitors from
Enniskillen, were involved. By the latter date the *Londonderry Sentinel* could
report: 'For this years celebration they came from almost every town and district in Northern Ireland to join with their brethren in the maiden city.'[112]

The shape, degree of support for and meaning of the siege of Derry have
undergone many changes over three centuries. During the late eighteenth and
nineteenth centuries most of the elements of celebration and ritual associated with the commemorations today fell into place. Many aspects of the modern siege celebration can be located to certain dates of origin. By the time

112 Neil Jarman, *Material conflicts: parades and visual displays in Northern Ireland* (Oxford, 1997).

of the bicentenary the commemorations in Derry had taken on most of the characteristics with which we associate these events today. However, the numbers involved in these annual celebrations were still very limited. The organisation of the Apprentice Boys of Derry was essential for the growth in popular support for these events. The majority of Apprentice Boys' parent clubs today date from only the 1840s or 1850s. Under their control, and due both to local factors and national issues, the siege celebrations grew in popularity. From a very low degree of support in the 1830s and 1840s the Derry commemorations had become well attended by the 1880s. At this stage, however, formal involvement in these annual parades was limited largely to Protestant residents of Derry. An important change of rules in the 1880s allowed the creation of local clubs, outside the city. While some growth in club numbers ensued in the following two decades, real expansion occurred only after 1921. From a figure of 9 parent and local clubs in 1889, numbers grew to 23 in 1923, 100 in 1939, 178 in 1971 and over 200 in 1989. It is only in the last seventy years that it can be said that these Derry commemorations enjoyed significant involvement from the wider Protestant and Unionist community in Northern Ireland. For members of that community, in their modern day situation, the story of Derry has served as a meaningful lesson in their political and religious lives. Clearly this is a great change from earlier centuries when the siege had served as a strong Protestant symbol for a limited number of people and an even greater change from when it had served as an inclusive symbol for Protestant and Catholic.

Commemoration of the siege of Derry is seen as a key element in the Protestant and Unionist sense of tradition. From observation of current celebrations of the event this is fair comment. At the same time it is important to realise that what is regarded as 'traditional' often does not come to us in an unchanging line, transmitted naturally, from the date of origin of the tradition or the event on which it is based. Organisations, people and events influence and alter the traditions which we use. In this case the organisation of the Apprentice Boys of Derry, the influence of churchmen and politicians, and events such as the setting up of the new Northern Ireland in 1921, all had a direct bearing on how the siege of Derry has been commemorated. Contemporary affairs can influence how popular a particular tradition can be. The siege of Derry has developed into an important tradition because, especially in this century, it has been viewed by more and more people as a symbol and source of inspiration which has been relevant to their time. The story of the siege of Derry has been seen as very significant by Unionists and Protestants of Northern Ireland, in light of the political and religious conflict in their society. Each generation has interpreted the siege in particular ways to suit their current needs. This understanding of the rise of the importance of the tradition of remembering the siege of Derry must not be seen as devaluing it for those who share it. Instead it shows that often what others may regard as antiquarian or a hang-over from the past is rooted in present reality. Such understanding emphasises the importance of traditional commemorations. At the same time it also warns against the belief that these traditions are unchanging and fixed in time, which can lead to a failure to adjust effectively to modern circumstances and new events.

There has been considerable debate among historians about the rise of such traditions. Some have emphasised the roots of these traditions while others have stressed the modern situation which affects the way the traditions are taken up and become widely accepted. Eric Hobsbaum has talked of the 'invention of tradition' and has interpreted the rise of traditions as a response in the late nineteenth century to modern developments in communication, industrialisation and the political enfranchisement of the mass of the people. In the Irish context, the importance of the origin of tradition as opposed to the importance of the new conditions has been emphasised in differing degrees by various historians. This study shows how various aspects of the Derry siege tradition fell into place during the eighteenth and nineteenth centuries, which accords with those who place emphasis on the strength of long standing traditions. At the same time, however, the small number involved in this tradition over most of the early period has been stressed. Numbers involved were more substantial by the late nineteenth century but it was only the political and religious conditions of post-1921 Northern Ireland that caused the larger Protestant and Unionist community to be actively involved. Therefore, modern conditions were vital for the spread and survival of this tradition. Even the emergence of the home rule crisis in 1885-6 and in 1912 was not enough to generate wide interest in the Derry story. In spite of general social, political and economic change, as emphasised by Hobsbaum, it was the particular circumstances of post-1921 Northern Ireland that caused greater participation in Derry commemorations, a growth which has continued to this day. Much more important for this growth of popular involvement than any strong sense of underlying historical consciousness or general change, has been the continuing relevance of the siege story in the religious and political situation in Northern Ireland, and the development and promotion of the Derry commemorations by various individuals and organisations, in particular, the clubs of the Apprentice Boys of Derry.